BILL THOMAS

Bill Thomas is a solicitor, journalist and broadcaster. His is probably the best known legal voice on radio, as he is heard every week somewhere in the country and most weeks on BBC Radio 2's *Jimmy Young Show* answering listeners' problems and putting the law into everyday language.

Apart from running his own practice in South London, he writes widely for trade and general interest magazines on most aspects of consumer and family law as well as being a consultant for retail and manufacturing companies, where he brings his expertise into their customer relations policy.

The Jimmy Young Show is a music and current affairs programme which is broadcast on BBC Radio 2 five mornings a week. It has an average of 8 million daily listeners. Jimmy Young talks to people in the news and introduces regular features such as medical advice, help for listeners on any subject and legal guidance.

QUESTIONS
OF LAW

BILL THOMAS

Hamlyn Paperbacks

QUESTIONS OF LAW
ISBN 0 600 35562 4

First published in Great Britain 1979
by Hamlyn Paperbacks
Copyright © 1979 by W. H. Thomas

Hamlyn Paperbacks are published by
The Hamlyn Publishing Group Ltd,
Astronaut House,
Feltham,
Middlesex, England

Made and printed in Great Britain by
Hazell Watson & Viney Ltd, Aylesbury, Bucks

CONTENTS

For Robinson, without
whom there would be no
Legal Beagle

INTRODUCTION

This book is written in as simple a way as I can manage; but the subject matter is far from simple. The questions are based on the many thousands which are sent in to Jimmy Young on his daily show on BBC Radio 2. I have had to be selective and answer those which come up time and again. The book is far from comprehensive; so do not despair if your problem does not appear – get skilled legal help, because nothing I have said is in any way a substitute for that. I have tried to answer the basic problem and to point in the right direction for further help.

I am grateful to everyone who has helped with the preparation of the book, with ideas, suggestions, and by reading proofs and typing. Above all, I must thank the listeners to BBC Radio 2 – both for listening and for writing in, for responding each week so quickly with information and help – and for putting me right when I go astray.

Finally, the law I am qualified to write about is that of England and Wales. Scotland and Northern Ireland have their own excellent legal systems; although a great deal of the law is the same, there are substantive differences which mean that anyone living in those countries should seek local legal help.

At the back of the book – on page 198 – is a Glossary explaining all the legal terms printed *like this*.

All the figures quoted are correct at the time of publication but many will, inevitably, change over the next year.

1
ACCIDENTS AND INJURIES

1 Recently I was up a ladder in the kitchen. I leant across to fix something to the wall and overbalanced. To save myself I grabbed at the wall-cabinet; to my horror this came away from the wall and crashed to the floor – with me following close behind! Surely the builder should have taken reasonable precautions to ensure that the cabinet was firmly fixed; it only had a small screw at each corner?

A. You really want the lot, don't you! It was your fault that you overbalanced. The builder cannot reasonably have foreseen that the cabinet would have been needed as a safety device. His method of fixing it might have been a bit better, but as it had kept the thing on the wall for a long time (which was what it was meant to do) you cannot really complain about the size of the screws. I am afraid that you have no claim at all – unless overbalancing was due to some defect in the *ladder*, in which case you may – just may – have redress against the person who sold it to you; or the manufacturer if you can show that he was to blame. And that's not easy.

2 Why shouldn't I be entitled to compensation from someone as of right?

A. This is one of my hobbyhorses. The law in this country is, briefly, that you can only get compensation in two instances. First, if the goods are new and go wrong – you may have a claim against the shop that sold them to you (under the contract – see question 145). Secondly, if the manufacturer – or someone else – is *to blame*. Dealing here with the second part, it is extremely difficult to establish blame so as to show that someone was *negligent*. There are different situations in which the same injury can be sustained but where the likelihood of compensation differs considerably. For instance, if you break your leg at home by falling off a ladder (and not being saved by the kitchen furniture!) the chances of proving that the ladder was negligently made are very slim; hence a poor claim for *damages*. If the leg is broken at work then your case is stronger, because you may be able to show that your employer had failed to provide you with a safe system of working, or had not taken adequate precautions to see that the place was safe and free from obstructions. If you were run over on a zebra crossing and broke your leg, then you are certain to have a claim. This really is stupid, but it is the law. The injury is the same; the needs of your dependants are the same; it seems illogical that your damages can range from nil to 100% just because someone was at fault. In New Zealand you would be compensated no matter *how* your injury was caused because the government there decided that the needs of the victim and his family were greater than the legal requirement of proving blame. Lawyers in the U.K. have not been impressed by the New Zealand scheme – because they feel that the law is so well established and understood that there is no need to interfere with it. And a recent Royal Commission which looked at the way injury compensation was worked out did not consider that any radical alteration in the fault-based system was appropriate. Tough, eh?

3 I was driving along a road, observing the speed limit and on the correct side, when a large dog came running into my path. I couldn't stop, or even swerve, as there were parked cars in the way. A lot of damage was done, to me, to the car – and to the dog. His owner was eventually traced and only said that the dog was always getting out. Have I any claim against the owner?

A. It all depends on whether the dog was simply left to his own devices by the owner or was kept securely but managed to escape. In the first case, the owner is almost certainly liable – especially if he knew that the dog was always straying. On the other hand, if the owner had done all that he reasonably could to keep the dog in, but the animal had used his guile for an escape plan, the owner may not be responsible. So if he had fenced the garden and had a gate with a sign saying 'please keep shut', and someone had come into the garden and left the gate open – the owner wouldn't be liable either.

4 Would it have been different if the dog was being walked along the pavement by the owner?

A. If the dog was off the lead the owner *would* be liable. If the lead was on but the dog had slipped out of his collar or the lead had snapped – then you might have a claim, but only if you could show that the owner knew, or ought reasonably to have known, that the collar or lead was dodgy. (Remember that it is an offence to allow a pet dog to be on a highway or in a place where the public go without a collar bearing the name and address of the owner.)

5 I was hit by a car which was driven on without stopping. No one was able to get the number of the car although several people actually saw the incident. My injuries kept me off work for several weeks and I now have a permanent limp as a result. I am not insured at all; how can I get compensation from the person responsible?

A. First of all, remember what I have written above about *blame*. Just because you were hit does not automatically give you a right to compensation. You must be able to show that the driver was to blame – at least in part. Secondly, you have no legal right to compensation if the driver cannot be traced, because he, and only he, is liable to you. But the insurance industry have set up a body called the Motor Insurers' Bureau (M.I.B.) which will deal with claims by victims of hit-and-run drivers. If you can satisfy the M.I.B. that the driver was responsible – and here the witnesses could be very important for you – then it *may* make an *ex gratia* payment to you. You have no *right* to this – but it is worth applying to the M.I.B. for your claim to be considered.

6 If the driver *was* traced but turned out to be uninsured will the M.I.B. help?

A. Generally speaking you will have to sue the offending driver and obtain judgment against him; only if he has no assets will you be able to look to the M.I.B. And they will only deal with death or injury claims – not with damage to your property. The M.I.B. has fairly strict rules which have to be followed, so if you discover early on (as you almost certainly will) that the driver is not insured, get on to the M.I.B. and find out what they want you to do. You will have a solicitor acting for you; remind him about the M.I.B.

7 While travelling by train between London and Worcester a passenger slammed the door of the compartment and caught the tip of my finger. Not only did I lose the joint, but also a lot of blood, which ruined my clothes. Other passengers were helpful but the railway staff didn't do much and my letter asking for injury compensation has been ignored.

A. British Rail may have ignored you because you have no claim. It's all a matter of *blame*. No railway employee slammed the door, it was the passenger who got off at Moreton-in-Marsh. *He* is the only one to blame.

8 I was getting off a train in a station. It had stopped and I was half-way out of the door when it suddenly lurched forward

about a foot, throwing me off balance and on to the platform. I landed on a pile of mailbags which broke my fall, but I twisted an ankle and hurt my arm, as well as tearing my clothes and stockings. A couple of postmen helped me to get my breath back. I don't know what to do about claiming. Whom do I write to?

A. British Rail deal with their own insurance matters and will process your claim. In theory they should have a record of the accident, but it is still up to you to prove your case and show that they were *negligent*. If you got the names and addresses of any witnesses, so much the better. You may be able to trace the two postmen, too, and find out if they saw what happened. You should write (keeping a copy) to the appropriate Area Manager (name and address from your local station) explaining what happened. Your letter will then be passed to the insurance division which will deal with it. You should also consider getting legal advice so that you can establish how much money you might expect to get.

9 My husband was killed at work. A machine he was working on became electrically live and he was electrocuted. I have three children under twelve. My husband had no insurance and did not belong to a union. Is it worth my trying to see if the firm will make an offer?

A. Yes – you must. It may well take a long time but you owe it to yourself and the children to do so. Go to a solicitor and apply for *legal aid* (see question 412). Even if you don't qualify for legal aid it is still worth making a claim – or at least doing the groundwork. Your husband's employers will have some difficulty in showing the safety procedures were working well. Of course there may have been a good and unforeseeable reason for this tragedy; or your husband may have caused it by doing something which he knew was unsafe, or outside the scope of his training or experience. But if you do not do anything you will never know.

10 I have been told that you cannot sue the nationalized industries for negligence and that the only money you get is because they feel morally responsible.

A. Not so. All nationalized bodies are liable in negligence for the acts or omissions of their staff. So if you are killed by a vehicle owned by the Post Office, or your house is blown up by a gas leak, or you are injured in a train or plane crash – you can sue the appropriate public body – provided, of course, that you can show that it is to blame. There is an exception for the Post Office as regards its functions over the post and telecommunications, but that does not extend to its civil liability in negligence for death or injury.

11 A friend of mine sued a driver who had injured her. The claim was settled with a payment which she was advised to accept by her solicitor. Now she finds – three years later – that it was not enough. It there any way of reopening the case?

A. Not a chance, I am afraid. The whole basis of the award of damages – whether by a court or on a settlement – is that it is a once-for-all payment. The Royal Commission on personal injury compensation suggested that part of an award should be by regular payments, instead of a lump sum, so that there could be revision up or down both to take inflation into account and and to enable a change in medical condition to be reviewed in money terms. It is, however, unlikely that this will be implemented. So you are stuck with whatever you get or settle for.

12 Do I have to prove negligence if I am injured at work?

A. Yes and no; if you can show that there was a breach of any of the many rules which impose obligations on employers to do things safely – the Factories Acts, the Health and Safety at Work Act, the Building Regulations, to name a few – then you can simply say that there was a *breach of statutory duty* and claim compensation for *that* without having to prove blame at all. Usually your solicitor will frame the claim to include negligence as well; belt and braces, if you like.

13 Recently I was driving normally when the car skidded on a bend and crashed. It was impossible to drive it so I had to call a garage mechanic out. The man said that mine was the fifth case that week and that the cause was a very slippery surface due to lack of maintenance by the highway authority. The bill was over £200 and although my insurance met it, I will lose my no-claims bonus. Have I any chance of a claim against the council?

A. Only if you can prove two things: first that the council had failed to maintain the road to a reasonable standard, and second that the council knew of the danger. You were the first person to tell the council and the incidents had all occurred within a short space of time; it could be said that they had not had a reasonable opportunity to inspect the road in a routine way; so you may have a difficult job. It is one of those cases where you will have to go some way along the suing track before you know just what the council did or did not know or do, unless they volunteer the information, of course. This is unlikely because you, as the victim making the claim, have to prove your allegations.

14 Walking along the pavement I tripped on a paving stone which was uneven and about half an inch below the level of the path. I hurt my knee and broke my glasses – which cost over £40 to replace. I wrote to the council but their insurance company told me that I had no claim because the unevenness wasn't bad enough, and the council couldn't look at every paving stone every day.

A. Unfortunately you may have been given correct information. Although the law was changed in 1961 with the intention of helping people who were affected by non-repair of paths and roads, there have been a couple of cases where the courts have held that, provided there was regular inspection and that the hole or depression was less than an inch, the claimant will not win. In one case, although the victim showed that lots of people knew of the poor standard of the path, no one had told the local council and she lost her case.

15 My son plays rugby and football. With the increasing violence in these games, I am worried that he will be hurt. If he is, could any claim be brought against anyone – the school or the other team?

A. As a general rule, people who play games accept the risks that are sometimes inevitable. If you play cricket, you may get a ball in the eye, or a bat on the head, by accident. And in all contact sports there is a risk of injury to limbs. But if another player deliberately breaks the rules and causes injury – a late tackle when the player is miles from the ball, or a trip or a kick on the head – the victim may well have a civil claim for damages under the law of trespass. A soccer player has been ordered to pay damages for a deliberate foul; I can see no reason why this principle shouldn't be extended. It might clear up some of the worst excesses.

16 What rules are used to award compensation for injuries? You read of huge sums being awarded to some people and what seem very small amounts to others. Can you explain?

A. The damages one gets are in two parts. *Special damages* are the money you have lost or spent – wages, medical expenses, travel, ruined clothes or vehicles. This is usually agreed by your solicitor and the other side, so that if you win there is no argument, you get that figure without having to spend hours arguing about the precise amount. *General damages* are the rest – money to compensate you for pain and suffering, loss of expectation of life, loss of amenity and enjoyment. This is what the court will award you having heard all the evidence and found in your favour. One important thing to understand is that the general level of damages in this country is low. The huge sums you read about are invariably for people who were very badly injured quite early in life, but who were high – or potentially high – income earners. Coupled with the likely cost of medical and nursing attention over many years, the damages can be very high. But these are very exceptional. The general run of the mill case results in damages of hundreds of pounds, a few thousands sometimes, but rarely more.

17 Is there any way in which one can tell how much the court might award?

A. There is a kind of tariff which is applied. It is quite unofficial and simply exists because there are reports of cases and awards for injury tend to follow similar previous ones. The loss of one eye merits about £5000; both eyes, perhaps £40,000 – not vast sums by any means. And leg or arm injuries, even though permanent, only receive £1000 or so. So, don't be misled by what you read in the papers; it is only the very exceptional case that hits the headlines anyway. And remember that the damages can be – and often are – reduced because of what you may have done towards causing the accident or injury. This is known as *contributory negligence* and often results in a substantial reduction of the award.

18 What about seat belts? I have read that the damages can be affected by not wearing them. Is this right?

A. Yes, indeed! A driver or front seat passenger (unless very fat or pregnant) will be treated as contributing to the injury if a seat belt is not worn. If the injuries could have been prevented entirely, the reduction will be 25% of the damages; if they would have been less severe, 15% will be taken off. So belt up or you will pay for it!

19 I slipped and fell in a shop recently and twisted an ankle. The shop staff were very helpful, but when I mentioned compensation they laughed and said that the accident was my own fault and there was no liability on their part. I would have thought that they would have to take some of the responsibility because the slip was caused by something greasy having been spilt on the floor.

A. There is an obligation on shopkeepers to show that they take reasonable steps to prevent spillages and that, if they happen, they have a workable system to clean up quickly. In one case, a woman who slipped on some spilt yoghurt was able to recover damages because it was shown that there was no speedy system to clean up this sort of mess in the particular shop; sometimes a spillage could remain unwiped for fifteen minutes. This decision means that shops must have an adequate procedure, especially in self-service places where there is an even greater risk of things being dropped by the customers.

20 How does a trader take reasonable precautions to make sure that people do not get injured? After all, they don't have to come into the shop, do they?

A. No, and if that is the trader's attitude, I am not surprised if they go elsewhere! Reasonable steps means making sure that spillages are wiped up quickly, that there is someone whose job it is to keep an eye on the floor, to make sure that broken areas are roped off, that steps or other hazards are clearly pointed out and that warnings are displayed. There are lots of cases where people in shops, hotels or pubs have injured themselves in search of a lavatory. Dark corridors should be lit; sudden bends or steps should be indicated by a

10

clear notice. Then it is up to the person to look out for himself. The trader should take care that staircase banisters are sufficiently close together to prevent a child slipping through, that floors are sound and reasonably free from obstructions. The court will take into account that people should look where they are going; a person who fell over a four-foot high pile of cardboard boxes on a supermarket floor failed to get compensation.

21 During the winter our front garden and the path was covered with snow. I tried hard to keep a patch clear so that we could get in and out, but it became slippery because it froze harder. A visitor decided to avoid the slippery bit and walked on the grass (or where the grass would have been but for over a foot of snow). In doing so he put a foot into the pond and was hurt. Does he have a claim against me?

A. As a householder you have to take care to ensure that your premises are reasonably safe, or, if you know they are not, to point it out to people visiting you. In other words, you should not allow traps, holes or hidden hazards to be unmarked. The pond would not have been such a hazard in normal weather because a visitor would have been able to see it, and would thus have no claim. In winter it could have become one if you had diverted the path across the pond! But you had done your best to provide safe access in bad conditions and no one would have a claim. Really *doing one's best* is the way to describe the duty of care which one owes to visitors.

22 Every fortnight I have my windows cleaned. I always have a nagging worry that if the window-cleaner falls off his ladder or misses his footing I could be liable. Is there any risk of liability?

A. Apply the *doing one's best* test. If you supply him with a ladder you know to be unsafe, he may claim against you in negligence, because you have not acted reasonably. But if he

11

falls from his own ladder that is his misfortune. If you suddenly discover that one of the ledges on which he usually stands is loose, again you may be liable *if* you don't tell him about it. But a gradual deterioration in your house which ends up in catastrophe does not of itself make you liable – unless you knew about it and failed to warn. The same thing applies to tradesmen generally. They are expected to possess a skill in their own line of work and if they come to a house to repair something they will be expected to appreciate that, certainly as far as whatever they are doing is concerned, all may not be entirely well or safe. They should take precautions themselves.

23 My mother was crossing the road; she reached the centre island and then began to cross the second half of the road. She was hit by a motor cyclist. There was a witness who said that the motor bike was going quite fast but that she had stepped out suddenly. I don't know what to do about claiming as she is bedridden.

A. You can employ a solicitor to act for your mother using the *Green Form* (see question 413) and he can obtain a *police report* and contact the witness. The trouble is, of course, proving that the motor cyclist *was* to blame. If your mother did just step out giving the man no chance, then there is no case. As the witness says that she did then that will tend to support the cyclist, a police report will also contain details of what the cyclist and anyone else who saw the accident had to say about it. It costs £10 to obtain from the Police Authority.

24 A trolley from a local supermarket ran down the pavement and hit my car. I complained to the manager who said that there was a limit to what he could do because people kept taking the trolleys out of the shop to carparks, etc., and he couldn't be held responsible. To be fair there was a lad trying to get the trolleys back inside. Have I a claim?

A. First, you may like to consider whether there is any criminal liability arising under a *bye-law* made by your local council. It won't help *you*, but it might do something to get the shop to improve its systems. Secondly you have the old, old problem of showing that the shop was to *blame*. Anyone could have left the trolley, or knocked it causing it to roll; and if the shop can show that it does have a recovery system – and you say that there was a lad there trying to do just that – they may well be able to satisfy the court that they tried their best, and so were not *negligent*.

25 I was travelling on a bus and had to stand because there were so many passengers. Just after the journey began the driver stood on the brakes and screeched to a halt. I was thrown down the aisle and hit my head on the front partition. I cut my face and broke my dentures. After treatment at hospital, I made a claim from the bus company, but they denied liability saying that the driver was trying to stop because a child ran into the road. But that doesn't deal with my injuries and time off work, does it?

A. No, it doesn't. But what did you want the driver to do – run the kid over? The driver was not negligent; he was not to blame; the person to blame was the *child*. You have no claim against anyone. Sorry.

26 Do I have a claim against the driver of a car whose passenger opens the car door and injures me as a pedestrian?

A. Almost certainly not – because it is nothing to do with the driver. Your claim is against the *passenger* because he was to *blame*.

27 Does this liability extend to pedestrians?

A. Yes, it does. In question 25, if the person who dashed

13

out into the road had been an adult, there might well be a claim against him by the person who was injured, as well as by the bus company for any damage to its bus. And a pedestrian who steps out in front of a motor cyclist, causing an accident, can be held fully responsible.

28 I took my car to a local service station to have it washed in a machine which you drive through. It came out minus its wing mirrors and one windscreen wiper blade. When I told the man in charge he said that it was always happening, and that he wouldn't use the machine himself. But there was also a notice up saying that the company wasn't liable for loss or damage arising from its negligence or for any other reason. Have I a claim and is it worth pursuing?

A. You have to show that the company was to blame. If they had a regular inspection system and maintained the machine properly so that the disappearance of the wing mirrors was an isolated event, you would not have a claim. But if they did not – and the comments by the man at the place indicate a history of damaged cars – you are on better ground.

The next hurdle is the notice containing the *exclusion clause*. This is not illegal; it may well still protect the company if it can prove that the exclusion clause is *reasonable*. Would you have used the machine had you known that you would have no come-back if your car was damaged? If the answer is yes – you won't have a claim because the exclusion clause *would* be reasonable. The trouble is that no one knows just what is or is not *reasonable*; so lawyers cannot advise with any certainty. This is very unsatisfactory. As to the value of bringing a claim – my advice is that it is always worth a stamp, but that any greater investment depends on the amount at stake.

29 Are retailers ever liable for injuries to their customers who bought goods which caused damage?

A. Yes. First, under the Sale of Goods Act, they will be liable to the person who bought the goods under the contract of sale because they will not be of merchantable quality or fit for their purpose. But that liability only extends to the person who bought the goods. There is no liability *in contract* to the buyer's family or anyone else who used them – because there was no contract. Secondly, they *may* be liable in negligence – if they have failed to check that what they sell is reasonably safe and properly made. This liability extends to *anyone* who uses the goods.

30 Is there any time limit in which to claim compensation for injuries?

A. Yes; it is generally three years from the date of the event which caused the injury. But there have been substantial changes in this basic rule, and it is now possible to bring an action within three years of the first date on which the victim realized that the injury existed. This may be many years later – and can cause substantial problems of *evidence* as records and witnesses may no longer exist, and memories will be even less reliable than usual.

31 A slate fell from my roof on to a passer-by. I didn't know that there was anything wrong with the roof – I think it must have been caused by the snow last winter. The chap was not badly hurt, but understandably was shaken. Does he have a claim against me?

A. Yes, he does. You must not injure people who are lawfully on the highway; if you do they will have a claim against you for *nuisance* or negligence. You will find that your house insurance policy – either for buildings or for contents – will almost certainly cover this liability, at least up to a substantial sum of money (often £250,000). So check that you are insured and that the policy extends to this sort of liability.

32 After a recent car crash, my seven-year-old vehicle was a write-off. It was insured for £1000 but will cost me £3500 to replace. My insurers have said that they will pay £500 as scrap value. I consider that the other driver was fully to blame and want to get the full replacement value. Have I a chance of doing this?

A. There is no chance whatever of getting the replacement value. Damages are assessed on the value of the article at the time it was damaged or destroyed. So the appropriate value would be what you had insured it for – £1000, or perhaps a bit less. *Your* insurance policy will contain a term saying that the company will pay the cost of repair or the write-off value, whichever is the lower. So it is perfectly entitled within its contract with you to pay only the £500 write-off value if it would cost more to repair the car. But your claim against the other driver is for the loss which you sustained – that is the £1000, plus any other expenses you incurred – car-hire, loss of wages, loss of profit, if you are in business. If you accept the £500 from your insurers, you could still claim the £1000 from the other driver. If you won you would have to repay your insurers the £500 they paid you – because you can't make a profit out of the accident.

33 I pulled up at a roundabout and a car went into the back of me; I was shoved forward and hit another car. Everyone blames someone else; the man who hit me says the road was dangerous. I am stuck with a damaged car that I can't afford to repair (it was insured for third-party only) and no one seems the least interested in doing anything.

A. You have to take the initiative. Just who *was* to blame? Were there any witnesses? Did the police come on the scene? Was anyone prosecuted? Find the answers to these questions and then see a solicitor and get some action going for you. Often the only way to resolve this sort of dispute is to issue a summons or a writ, and to do this your solicitor needs all the evidence that can be gathered together to ensure that there is someone who can be sued. If no one was, or no one can be found, tough. The loss is down to you.

2

DIVORCE AND
FAMILY PROBLEMS

34 How do I get a divorce? I have been married for several years and have two children aged eight and eleven. My husband and I just don't get on and live our own lives virtually independently.

A. To get a divorce you need to have been married. That may sound facetious, but it isn't meant to be. You would be surprised at the number of people who think they are married but are not; or those who are bigamously married; or have lived together for so long that they think they *are* married. Next, you need to have been married for at least three years. You can reduce that period in certain cases (see question 84). Finally, you need to have lived in England and Wales for at least one year (see question 85). Divorce is dealt with by any Divorce County Court and there will be one near you. The only ground for divorce nowadays is that the marriage has *irretrievably broken down* (see question 35). Because of the withdrawal of legal aid proper for divorce, you have to do the procedure and paperwork yourself although you may qualify for help from a solicitor under the *Green Form* (see question 413). If there is no contest you will not, in a normal case, have to go to court to get the divorce itself, although you will have to see a judge about the arrangements for the children. This is done in private and is fairly informal. The final decree is available six weeks after the divorce.

35 How do I show that the marriage has broken down?

A. By proving one or more of the following things: that your spouse has committed adultery and you find it intolerable to live with him or her; that your spouse has behaved in such a way that you cannot reasonably be expected to live with him or her (which is the long way of saying 'cruelty'); that your spouse has deserted you for at least two years; that you have lived apart for two years and you both agree to a divorce; finally, that you have lived apart for five years. Here you don't need to get the consent of your spouse – and indeed, can get divorced even if he or she does not want to and even if you caused the break up.

36 Can you go through these five instances in greater detail?

A. Yes. Adultery. This means sexual intercourse with someone to whom you are not married at a time when you *are* married to someone else. You also have to say this adultery makes it 'intolerable' for you to live with your spouse. The fact that you are applying for a divorce is plain evidence of that. If you didn't mind adultery, you would save your time and money – and marriage. If you discover about the adultery, but go on living with each other for more than six months, you will NOT be able to use that adultery as a ground for divorce.

37 What about 'unreasonable behaviour' as it has become known?

A. That is almost identical to the old-fashioned ground of cruelty. Again, if you have lived together for six months after the last incident of behaviour on which you hope to rely, you cannot apply for a divorce on this ground. What is unreasonable behaviour? Any violence, of course; and this may be a reason for applying within the three years (see question 84); sexual deviation, unless you happily take part in it; nagging; being deliberately kept short of money; drunkenness; unpleasant personal habits; silence; undue

19

selfishness; disregard of the children. If some of these apply to you then – providing there is no contest – you will probably have no trouble. It is a help if you can have corroborative evidence, say from your doctor – but this is much less important now one does not have to go to court. If there is a defended case or if the court say they want more supporting evidence then you may need to ask your doctor for a report.

38 What is desertion?

A. It is living apart *without* agreement. So if you say you are leaving and your spouse calls after you 'and a good job too', this will not be desertion, because there was an element of consent. It happens when one spouse just leaves and the other wants him/her to stay. It is less important now than it once was because of the new ground of two years' separation and consent. It is also possible to have a thing called *constructive desertion*. This happens when you walk out because you can't stand it any more. In other words, your spouse has behaved so badly or unreasonably that you are justified in leaving. The law says, in such a case, that the one who *stays* is the one in desertion. The test of behaviour justifying leaving is much the same as for the new type of 'cruelty' and you would have to spell out what you are complaining of. But desertion itself is NOT *unreasonable behaviour*.

39 Now these new ideas of separation and consent and so on. Just how do they work, and what is separation exactly?

A. First, the two years one. The ground is that you have lived apart for two years and the other side consents to a decree of divorce. The consent can be withdrawn at any time up to the 'hearing' of the divorce (that is, the day on which the divorce petition comes before the court – even though neither husband nor wife is present). The consent has to be given to the court in writing signed by the person being divorced. If you become reconciled for more than six months the two years CANNOT be used as a ground for divorce.

Secondly, the five years one. The *only* fact that has to be proved is that the parties have *lived apart* for at least that time. It doesn't matter if the person being divorced does not agree, or thinks it was the other's fault, or wants to make some allegations of his/her own. The fact of separation is all that the court is concerned with. This often causes distress to a person being divorced because it seems unfair or unreasonable. The definition of *living apart* is also very important. It means what it says. Very often the parties are unable to find two homes and so go on living in the same house. Is this 'living apart'? It almost certainly is providing the husband and wife *do* keep themselves to themselves. Each should cater, and housekeep, for himself; there should not be shared chores like laundry or shopping; separate beds are essential, or better still, separate rooms.

40 Several times you have mentioned 'proving' things; how does one do this?

A. By saying so – either in the witness box, on oath, or by making a sworn statement (an *affidavit*) in which this fact is said to be true. Remember that most divorces are now dealt with through the post, without the attendance of either party. And what you put in your divorce petition will be believed unless someone turns up and says it is not true. Only if your spouse consents to the divorce will the facts you are relying on being to be doubted.

41 How does one prove that separation has taken place? Do you need to see a solicitor or register the date?

A. No; it is an event which you *prove* by putting it in your divorce petition and then repeating it in the witness box or in your affidavit. Obviously, it is an idea to make a note in your diary for your own purpose; but you can almost always remember the date you moved out or the day your spouse told you he was leaving. If it was a long time ago you can simply say that it was 'in the month of May 1973', or 'some time during 1969', or even 'shortly after the end of the war on a date which the petitioner cannot remember'. The court will accept this once it is formally proved in the ways I have mentioned.

42 This five year separation – can anyone start off the divorce, even if he/she is the guilty one?

A. First – get the idea of guilt out of your head. The *irretrievable breakdown* concept was introduced to do away with the old business of blame or guilt. The court now recognizes that it takes two to make a marriage and to end it; and that adultery or desertion is usually symptomatic of some much greater weakness in the relationship. So anyone can bring proceedings for divorce on the five-year separation basis, even if he/she was the one who left or started living with someone else, or if the couple have been apart for many years.

43 What is the procedure for starting off a divorce case?

A. Well, you have to *qualify* in the ways I set out in question 34. You need a form of divorce petition, plus some copies. If you have children you need another form called the *statement of arrangements* form, together with some copies. And you must have your marriage certificate (or a certified copy from St Catherine's House (see page 207) if you were married in England or Wales). You have to fill in the forms – getting help from an advice worker or a solicitor under **Green Form** (see question 413) if necessary. Then you need copies of the petition; one for the court, one for your spouse and one for any other person whom you may name in the petition as having committed adultery with your spouse. The children's form contains details of where the children live, go to school, how they are maintained and what is done about access. You have to enter details of each child who is under eighteen and at school or in full-time education – so even apprentices or college students are included. A copy of this form is needed for the court and one for your spouse. You need copies of each for yourself, too, of course.

44 Next stage?

A. You send to a divorce county court – any one you like, but normally your nearest one (or Somerset House, if you live in Inner London) (see page 205) the following:
  · Petition and a copy for each person named
  · Children's arrangements form and a copy for your spouse
  · Marriage certificate
  · A fee of £20 payable to 'H.M. Paymaster General' (or 'P.R.F.D.' in cases started at Somerset House)
The fee can be *waived* if you are receiving Supplementary Benefit or Family Income Supplement or are getting Green Form help from a solicitor.

The court will arrange for the petition to be 'served' – that is sent to your spouse and anyone else – by post.

45 I don't know where my spouse is. Some people say that this stops me getting a divorce. Is this so?

A. No. You will have to try and trace him and then tell the court what you have done. Husbands can sometimes be traced through the D.H.S.S. computer – so it is helpful if you know his full names, date of birth and National Insurance Number. The court will write to the D.H.S.S. and see if they have details. If you do not know the date of birth or National Insurance number, and have a common name – like Thomas, for instance – it is very unlikely that D.H.S.S. records will be able to help. You can also make other enquiries, from trade union offices, employers – even the phone

23

book, for that can reveal all sorts of people. But if all this fails to find him, you can ask the court to make an order doing away with the need to serve the documents on your husband. (The same applies if your wife has left.)

46 My husband says that he won't have anything to do with a divorce, and if the papers are sent to him he will just throw them away. My friend says that this will mean I can't get divorced.

A. If I had a pound for every time I had heard the words 'my friend says' I should be lying in the sun somewhere! Try not to be influenced by what other people say – unless they are legally qualified or experienced. When the court sends the papers off to your spouse they include a form of receipt – an *acknowledgment of service* – which should be signed and returned to the court. Doing this does not compromise the person; it is a receipt and proof that the papers have been served; it also saves costs. If he simply throws them in the bin, and the court does not get the receipt, it will write to you and say so. You then ask for the court to arrange for personal service – that is, a court officer will find your spouse and hand the papers over face to face. There is an additional fee payable for this. Or you can employ a private detective to do so – which will cost money (often payable by the erring spouse in the end).

47 And will the court then accept the position?

A. Certainly; it has power to make an order saying that the person has received adequate notice of the divorce petition and is so deemed to have been served; or it can say that further steps to try and serve personally can be dispensed with.

48 This business of doing divorce by post; is it really possible to deal with the procedure – which seems to me to be quite complicated – without ever going to court?

A. I agree with you that the procedure *is* complicated. Although the forms and the steps to be taken have been simplified very considerably in the last few years, one should remember that divorce is a legal process and that there are rules which have to be followed. In a nutshell, what happens is this: petition – service – proof of service – verification of the facts in the petition by a sworn statement – request for the divorce to be dealt with by a judge in the open court in the absence of the parties – decree nisi – decree absolute. Having children means that you will have to see a judge in person. The only exceptions to this general rule are when there are complications about your nationality, the children or the facts you set out; or if your spouse defends the case.

49 I don't understand the difference between the *decree nisi* and the *decree absolute*. What does it mean?

A. The marriage is ended by the judge making an order of decree nisi. Nisi is Latin for 'unless'; and it means that the marriage is ended 'unless' someone turns up to say that it shouldn't be. For example, you might have made the whole thing up, or made statements that were not true – like you had lived apart when you had not; or you may still become reconciled. So there is a period of six weeks while you are in a sort of limbo – divorced but not free to remarry. After the six weeks you can ask the court to 'make the decree absolute'. This must be requested in writing by the person who is the petitioner.

50 Is it possible to expedite the decree absolute?

A. In theory, yes; but now that the period between nisi and absolute is only six weeks, the court is very reluctant to make it any shorter.

51 My wife divorced me some time ago; the court sent me copies of the various orders and the decree nisi. I now wish to

remarry but there is no decree absolute; apparently my ex-wife doesn't want to apply for it. It is stopping me from establishing a new life. What can I do?

A. The law says that the main person to apply for the decree absolute is the person to whom it was granted – usually the petitioner. But if he/she does not do so, then the other person may apply to the court for the absolute, after three months from the earliest date on which the decree absolute could have been granted (that is, four and a half months from the decree nisi). You have to give notice of this application to your ex-spouse.

52 What happens if you marry after the decree nisi but before the absolute?

A. First of all, it is difficult to do this unless you deliberately deceive the registrar to whom you apply for remarriage because he will ask you if you have been married before. If you said 'yes', he would need to see the decree absolute; if you said 'no' . . . well, no more need be said. But if by some misunderstanding you *did* remarry, then the second marriage would be bigamous, and you should take legal advice immediately. You could apply for the original decree to be made absolute and then get remarried again. This would regularize your relationship. Or you could apply to the court for a declaration that the bigamous marriage was a mistake and was void, before marrying again.

53 Does the reconciliation of a husband and wife after decree nisi but before absolute have any bearing on the divorce?

A. It does indeed. If the living together lasts for more than six months then the rule about separation being brought to an end (see question 39) applies. The absolute will not be made because the marriage will be treated as *not* having broken down irretrievably after all – even though the reconciled relationship may deteriorate after the six months. So you are still married, and would have to start all over again for a divorce on new grounds.

54 Money. As a wife whose husband has left and is living with someone else, can I expect him to maintain me?

A. It all depends. This question, which is so important to many, many women, is a tricky one to deal with except on the basis of general rules which often are of little value because of the individual circumstances of the people involved. But here goes. A wife can usually expect to receive for *herself* about one third of the joint incomes of herself and her spouse.

Example: husband   £5000 p.a. gross (before deductions)
          wife   £1000 p.a. gross
Joint incomes = £6000
One third   = £2000
Deduct wife's pay   £1000
              £1000 maintenance from husband

If there is a house on mortgage for which the husband pays the instalments then this figure of £1000 will be adjusted, so much depends on the special facts of the case. One way of thinking about a wife's maintenance is to see that if a wife earns more than *half* her husband's pay she will usually not get anything. If she earns less than half, she probably will get something.

55 Does this include what the children receive?

A. Maintenance for children is always treated separately. While a wife may or may not qualify for money herself, the father is always under a legal obligation to support his children. How much is paid depends on what his earnings are, how many children there are and what his responsibilities may be. A usual figure may be between £7 and £12 per child per week – but obviously a man who is paid £70 per week, has re-married, has children by both unions, and is maintaining his first wife would be unable to cope with that sort of figure. The best way is to try and negotiate a suitable figure; if this can't be done, then the court is there to do the calculating.

56 The house in which I live is the matrimonial home and it is at present in my husband's name. He tells me that I have no share in it and that he can get me out. I have been married for fifteen years and we have three children. Is he right? Would it make any difference if the house were in joint names?

A. Your husband is in for a shock. Since 1973 the law has enabled the court to make whatever order it thinks will do justice between the parties to a marriage. So it can change the ownership from his name to yours alone; into joint names; direct that the house be held until the youngest child grows up, then be sold. Virtually anything can be done, irrespective of whose name is on the deeds. That's the first point. Secondly, of course you have a share. Although the law seems to say that one starts from the basis that a wife gets a third, many cases these days decide that the property should be shared equally.

57 I am worried that the house will be sold over our heads by my husband because he is anxious to get his hands on the money.

A. It is quite difficult to do this. But if you fear that it may be done, you can prevent an actual sale from being concluded by protecting your interest and registering a special *land charge* or 'notice' at one of the departments of the *Land Registry,* depending on whether or not the title to the land is registered. It only costs £1 to do this; 50p if the land is registered. You will find that the Land Registry will provide you with information and guidance, but not advice.

58 Earlier on you stated that one cannot get divorced until the marriage has lasted three years. Does this also apply to maintenance and so on?

A. No; you can apply to a magistrates court (see question 82) for orders for maintenance and most things related to a marriage (e.g. custody, separation order) at *any* time after the marriage. Or you can apply for maintenance in a divorce county court under Section 27 of the Matrimonial Causes Act 1973 on the ground that your husband has *wilfully neglected to maintain* you or the children. This application can be made at any time, too, and is not dependent on the three-years rule.

59 Has the concept of blame/guilt really been abolished and does it not have some relevance to maintenance?

A. In a fringe way it just might. The law does require the judge to 'have regard to the conduct' of the parties when making financial orders. But unless a wife has flagrantly abandoned her children leaving the husband in the lurch; or deliberately waited until a house was put into their joint names while having an affair, and then walked out claiming her share – the usual rules will be applied to divide the matrimonial assets reasonably fairly.

60 As a husband I simply cannot afford to pay all the things that my wife wants. She is looking after the two children and doesn't work. I pay the mortgage, rates and the bills, I also pay her a lot each week. I can barely afford to rent a room and certainly have nothing to look forward to, as I couldn't possibly expect a woman to take me on with these financial burdens.

A. The first and hardest rule to learn is that one person's pay packet will not support separate homes – unless you are very well off, or lucky. Secondly, a wife who does not work for genuine reasons – very young pre-school-age children, ill-health, old age – is *entitled* to look to her husband for support; and with children she is *entitled* to money for them until they finish their education. If this means, as it often does, that the man is left with less than half his pay, then that is life; it is hard, but there are three mouths to feed on her side as against his one. So it is not unreasonable that she is getting the lion's share of such bread that is being won. Men often complain to me about this 'unfairness'; I am sorry, I don't see it as unfair at all, but as a consequence of the break-up of the marriage. Someone has to support the dependents; the man earns and is able to do so. Therefore, he should accept it and pay up.

61 That is all very well, but my ex-wife just won't work, claiming that jobs don't exist, and that the children – who are all at school – are too young.

A. Judges will expect young women to work these days. And they will require compelling evidence to show why they do not work. If they conclude that the woman is just relying on a meal-ticket from her former husband they can award her money as if she had been at work – leaving her to do something to earn the balance.

62 I live with a divorced man and, of course, contribute to our joint finances. The money I pay goes directly to his first wife who sits in the matrimonial home not working while I subsidize her. I think this is most unfair. Why should it be allowed?

A. You are wrong about subsidizing the former wife. Her maintenance payments are related to her ex-husband's income. Your financial contribution to the new household is only relevant to the extent that your man can claim only half what it costs him to live with you as an expense (because you will be paying the other half). The feeling which you have is one of bitterness; no doubt the ex-wife feels uncharitable about you. So long as bitterness exists, there is little hope for a reasonable arrangement being worked out.

63 It's all very well for you to say that; it's not your money and house being taken away from you. The lawyers on both sides often urge their clients to go on fighting anyway as far as I can tell. What would you do in this situation?

A. Lawyers are in a difficult position. They are trained to take part in an 'adversary activity' – that is, one in which you promote the best interests of *your* client and attempt to defeat what the other side claims or wants. So if a client says that she has sorted everything out with her spouse and just wants it approved by the court, but the solicitor knows that she is not getting what a court would have awarded (or if a husband is paying over the odds), he will feel obliged to advise his client of that fact. Then the parties begin to think that all is not quite as desirable as they believed, and the needle can start its insidious slide inwards. I have known such compromises end up in hard-fought battles just because of the involvement of the lawyers – both of whom believed, I am quite sure, that they were doing the best for their clients. What I should like to see is both parties being made to have an interview with the solicitor on the other side so that each can learn what happens if the boot were on the other foot. This is just my own view, of course; but I think it could help put money and housing in perspective sometimes, especially when emotions have taken over from reality. Occasionally I will be asked to see both husband and wife who have separated and try to explain to them both what sort of financial arrangement might be worked out by a judge if they went on to the end. (I cannot act for either of them and so can be completely unbiased.) This can be a help.

64 It has been suggested to me that one way of carving up the property is to put it all down on a piece of paper and agree all the terms, then ask the court to make a 'consent' order. Is this a good idea?

A. A *consent* order is what it sounds like – an arrangement between people embodied in and having the force of a court order (as though the judge had made it at the end of a contest). For many things it is beneficial – tax advantages to both sides, very often, and it means that the money side – at least for the wife – is settled. However, and this is the one problem, where financial arrangements for a wife are finalized in a consent order – her maintenance and perhaps the rearrangement of the ownership of the house – you *cannot* appeal to get the order changed if there is a subsequent variation in either person's finances. You can negotiate, of course, and this quite often happens; but a once-for-all financial order made by consent cannot be reopened. The only exception is money for the children – which can always be referred back to the court.

65 What tax advantages are there?

A. This is best dealt with under tax generally (see questions 380 to 385).

66 Whatever kind of order you get, how can you make sure that the man pays?

A. There is no way known to man to make someone pay money if he doesn't want to. There are things you can do to protect yourself, but at the end of the day it requires the co-operation of the person ordered to pay. A maintenance order made in a county court can be *registered* in a magistrates court for the area in which the person having to pay lives. He then makes his payments direct to that magistrates court. If he doesn't pay or gets into arrears, the magistrates court can be asked to enforce the payment. If he moves one has to start again. In some cases the court can be asked to make an *attachment of earnings* order, which directs his employer to deduct the maintenance from his pay each week or month and send it to the wife. Fine in principle, but there

32

are quite stringent financial limits which make this procedure useless in cases of low wage earners; again, if he changes
jobs you have to start all over again. And if the man is self-
employed it is almost impossible to extract the money if he
won't pay willingly.

**67 My wife and I have been separated for over twenty years,
and I have always sent her money after she got a magistrates
order in 1960. I am going to divorce her on the two-years
separation ground, but she has told my son that she will block
this because of the hardship she will be caused financially. I
thought the right to a divorce was automatic in this sort of
case. She can't stop my divorce, can she?**

A. Generally, she can't prevent you getting a decree nisi,
because you have been apart for over five years. In order to
give some protection – though to be fair, not much – to
wives who are divorced against their will, the law says that
there is a right for a wife to go to the judge and try and
satisfy him that there will be grave financial hardship
caused by the divorce. The judge *can* throw the petition out,
but virtually every time he will direct that the husband makes
adequate provision (within his means) for the wife and
allow the divorce to proceed on this basis. The wife can
also apply after decree nisi for the money side to be reviewed
so that the judge can say if it is fair, or the best that can be
worked out. Pension rights are also looked at; a wife who is
divorced in her fifties loses various rights to pensions on her
husband's contributions – and the court will sometimes order
that he takes out a policy of insurance to protect her. Everything depends on the particular circumstances, but in answer
to your question, it is possible, very occasionally, to block a
divorce.

**68 My former wife has had a maintenance order for £10 per
week for many years. I am about to retire and my whole
financial situation will change, because I will just have the**

state pension eked out by my savings. I will not be able to afford the £10, though I appreciate that my ex-wife will also need to be supported. What can I do? Should I simply reduce the payments?

A. That would be fatal, because immediately arrears would start to build up and you would be looked at with disfavour as someone who was shirking his responsibility. No, what you should do is apply to the court to 'vary' the original maintenance on the basis that your circumstances have changed. This has to be done by giving notice to your ex-wife obviously, and then each of you will be able to give details of your situation to the court. Or you could try an informal approach to the other side, explaining the problem and see if they will agree to a variation by consent. In any case you would do well to get legal advice. But *don't* just reduce the payments off your own bat.

69 The youngest child for whom I paid maintenance has now left school and is working. The order provided for £8 per week until 'age seventeen or further order'. My daughters' mother seems to think I will go on paying this. Should I?

A. The form of words means that until your daughter reached the age of seventeen or until the order was changed in some way, you would have to pay. But once that age is attained you can stop; if there is some reason why payment should continue after then, it is up to the child's mother to go back to the court – but if the girl is working it is difficult to see any reason to make you go on paying.

70 I was ordered to pay money to my ex-wife. She has now remarried, I have discovered, and I am still paying. I did mention to her that I thought it was up to her new bloke to support her, but got a short answer.

A. If the money you pay is *for* the wife (and NOT for the children) then your obligation to pay it ceases immediately on her remarriage. So you can stop the payment immediately. If there are arrears outstanding from before her remarriage, you should take steps to pay them off. Any money payable to your children, on the other hand, remains payable until the age limit is reached.

71 Is it possible for the mortgage on the house to be transferred into my wife's name? I am paying the instalments at present, but I hope that an arrangement will be made whereby she takes it all over and I will give her my share in the house. The only problem is the mortgage; I don't know what the building society will do.

A. For heaven's sake, ask! It is *very* important to realize that the building society has an interest in the house and is concerned to know that the instalments will be paid, and that arrears will not be allowed to build up. Very often the first the society knows about a marriage break-down is when they are told during proceedings they have started for possession – the instalments having stopped and their letters having been ignored. An early discussion with the local manager can save considerable worry and expense. It may be suggested that you switch to an *option mortgage*. So, put it high on your list of things do to at the very outset. Whether it will be possible to do what you want depends on the wife's financial situation after the proposed arrangement has been completed. If she will be able to pay the instalments on the income she will have, the society will probably agree. But often a further loan is required to 'buy out' the spouse who has left. This obviously means that the instalments will increase, and the society will need to be quite certain that this higher commitment is within the wife's reach. So a guarantor may be needed. And, in any event, don't blithely go ahead with plans – by consent or otherwise – without taking the society fully into your confidence. You may be in for a shock if you do.

35

72 Following my divorce my wife was awarded custody of the children with 'reasonable access' to me. She and I can't agree on what reasonable means. Are there any guidelines, and what can I do to get the access arrangements sorted out?

A. A *reasonable access* direction is normally made in the hope and expectation that the parents will be able to work out what is suitable. If this sort of negotiation doesn't produce an agreed plan, you can apply to the court for directions as to what access should be allowed. A fairly normal access arrangement is for the parent to see the children every other weekend – the whole of Saturday and Sunday, perhaps – with two weeks in the summer and a week in the Christmas and Easter holidays, with the actual festivals alternating between parents. A lot depends on where you live, of course. A court is reluctant to lay down a time-table, unless no other course is possible – because it is a court order, and failure to comply with it may be contempt. And each parent may try to adhere to the thing to ludicrous degrees – 'he was five minutes late bringing Jasper home'; 'Sharon has a cold so you can't see her this weekend; the order says every other one, so you will have to wait a month' – this is the despair of all people who care about children, because one parent is just using the children to get at the other, often for reasons which are completely irrational. What is at stake is 'the best interests of the children' – not the satisfaction or vindictiveness of the parents. So – try and get some form of agreement to work; if it can't be done, apply to the court. The judge may ask for a report by a social worker, who will see both parents, anyone with whom they live, the children, and possibly the schools, and then make recommendations. This report will be made available to you and your former spouse.

73 What is access intended to do? I find it very difficult, because each time just as one is beginning to get on good terms with the children, they have to go back; and there is very little one can do except go to museums, zoos and the pictures.

A. I feel for you. For access to mean anything there is a great deal of hard work needed – by you and the children. The object is to enable the parent who is separated from them to keep in touch with the children. If you can, try to establish normality in your plans. In a normal family, outings may be treats; so keep them as treats on access weekends. If you have space at home, get the children to keep toys, books and games at your place – so that there is a nucleus of home-based activity. Encourage homework, television and football just as you would if they lived with you. Try to avoid all discussion about the other parent, except about non-contentious things. The lack of money, or her boy-friends, or his new car should be avoided like the plague. Finally, remember that children are people; they have feelings, thoughts and ideas – and they can quickly work out the best way to manipulate their parents, including play-ing one off against the other – 'Mummy lets me light the fire'; 'Daddy lets me stay up till *Match of the Day*' – will be heard from time to time. It can be quite effective to challenge these assertions and ask the child if he minds if you check this with the other parent.

74 Does the judge take any account of the children's views? My elder son, who is fifteen, doesn't want to see his mother, at least not regularly.

A. Certainly, the older the child the more the notice that is taken; judges sometimes see the children in private to assess their views about their parents. And, of course, an older child cannot be forced to go anywhere against his will. Sometimes it is difficult to tell to what extent the child's wishes reflect what he has been told by one or other parent. Also children tend to have their own activities, sport, scouts, youth club, a Saturday job – all of which can impinge on what would otherwise be access time; and it is unfair to put the burden of choosing between these things and seeing Dad all the time. Equally, there is no reason why a teenager should not think of others, too.

75 I don't want my former husband to bring my children into contact with his mistress. Can I stop this happening?

A. It is better if you try not to use emotive words like 'mistress'; and remember that they are not YOUR children – they are his, too. There was a time when the courts would prevent children having contact with a parent who was living with someone to whom he/she wasn't married. But these days there can be no objection to a child seeing his parent in his own domestic setting – and if that includes a new partner, that is a fact of life. The burden which is placed on the new partner is often overlooked. It is a very difficult course to steer between being taken as a usurper of the position of the ex-spouse, or as an indifferent nonentity. In fact, the new partner, male or female, can play an important part in the lives of the children, because if the relationship develops, the children may be able to talk about problems which they would never be able to discuss with their parents. So, much depends on the willingness of the partner and the children to get on good terms. When it works it is a tremendous achievement of great value to the children. Remember, too, that in any event as your children grow up they make their own friends and amusements, and you have less and less say in what they do and whom they meet. They are not devoid of judgment and can work out whom they like and whom they don't. It is wrong to try and control whom they are allowed to come into contact with.

76 Now that I have remarried my husband and I want to adopt the children by both our previous marriages. Then we feel we will be a real family. How do we set about doing this?

A. There is a recent change in the law which effectively prohibits any such adoption. An application to an adoption court by a parent and step-parent will be dismissed because the law says that custody, etc., should be dealt with by the court. I suppose that the divorce court might decide that adoption *was* in the interests of the child, in which case you could try for an order. The reasoning behind this change was to ensure continuity of contact and identity between the child and his natural parent, which would be lost if there were an adoption – where the rights of the real parents are shut out for ever. Even if the other parent agrees to an adoption you will still face problems.

77 I have lived with a man for many years although we are not married. I am worried that if we break up my position might not be very strong.

A. As far as maintenance is concerned, you are right. You have no rights like those of a wife to claim financial support. If you have children who are under eighteen you can get money for them from your man. If you live together in a house which is in his name, you have a right to apply for a share of it. Recent decisions have given *common-law wives* a reasonably fair share of the house. So if you do break up and are threatened with eviction, do see a solicitor straight-away and ask for advice on your rights. And don't forget that a common-law wife has the same rights to claim money from the estate of her dead partner as a wife does (see question 279).

78 We live in a council house which is in my husband's name. Our marriage has been dead for years; we only stayed together for the children. Now he says that he is going to divorce me and wants me out of the house. Why should I be expected to leave my home?

A. One answer to that is, why should *he*? It is in his name, he pays the rent. You are both adult without dependent children; if your marriage breaks down that is unfortunate, and obviously one of you will have to find somewhere else to live. If your husband is violent, the court will be able to consider turning him out. But that apart, why should he be under any greater obligation to go than you? The rules I mentioned about transferring property do not apply to council tenancies where there is a rule against changing ownership, so the court may not be able to make any order changing the tenancy even if it wanted to. Much will depend on the attitude of the local council.

79 My former wife is making all access arrangements difficult, and even though the court has made an order she is turning the children against me, with the result that they don't want to come and stay. Even the welfare officer agrees that the access is not working well. Is there anything I can do?

A. There are situations where the only thing that matters – that is, the interest of the children – is best served by one parent cutting off altogether. This is, of course, a terribly difficult decision to make, but if the alternative is years of difficulty, hostility and resentment coupled with an increasing reluctance on the part of the children to see, let alone stay with, a parent, such a decision may be inevitable. The parent who makes it may feel that when the children are grown up they will feel sufficiently curious to seek out and get to know the parent whose name has been blackened. Because that is likely to happen, too.

80 Can I take the children to Scotland for a holiday? I was awarded custody some years ago, but I have now been told that I cannot take the children away, even for a day trip to France.

A. Once a court order has been made relating to custody, the child cannot be taken *out of the jurisdiction* of the court in England and Wales. This means that you cannot go to Scotland, Ireland (North or South), or any where else without asking the court for permission. You also need the consent of the other parent, which may be refused. If that happens, you can apply formally to the court on giving notice to the other side, setting out where, why and for how long you are going. But if you and the other parent agree, you can make a general agreement that either of you can take the child abroad on your promise to bring him back if called upon to do so. This is sent to the court. It may seem a bit far-fetched, but remember that the courts of England and Wales can only deal with matters arising within their jurisdiction; you cannot make someone do something in a foreign country by an English court order – and once the child has gone, that may be that.

81 How do I get a legal separation?

A. This is one of the commonest questions that a solicitor is asked. In fact, there isn't really any such thing. You can go to a magistrates court and apply for an order for maintenance, custody of children or access if you can show that your spouse has deserted you, committed adultery, been cruel to you or a child, or has failed to maintain you or the children. And the court can include an order that you should no longer have to live together (a non-cohabitation clause). But there is no power to make what is often called a *separation order* or a *legal separation* – although this may well be the effective end product of your application to the court.

82 How do I make an application to a magistrates court?

A. You can employ a solicitor on *legal aid* or on *Green Form* (see question 413); or you can do it yourself by going to the court for the district in which you live and *making a complaint*; the court staff will provide you with the appropriate forms and will give some guidance – but *not* advice. The procedure is cheaper and – in some cases – quicker than that in the county court, and there is the advantage that you don't have to wait for three years to go by, as you do for a divorce. But the magistrates cannot make an order turning a spouse out of the house if he is violent (see the next question), nor can they deal with house property matters. Which court you choose really depends on your ultimate plans; if you want a divorce, then you might as well go to the county court and get the whole thing sorted out. If money is all that you are after, the magistrates court is there.

83 I haven't been married long – certainly not long enough to get a divorce, but I am frightened of my husband. He tries to attack me, often quite unexpectedly; and he seems to get fits of violence.

A. There has been a very important improvement in the law which now enables wives (and unmarried people too) to seek the help of the court in a domestic violence situation. You can get *legal aid* or *Green Form* advice (see question 413) and make an urgent application to any divorce county court. The judge can make a number of orders to help you, once you have established the basis for your fear – either of actual violence or threats. These range from an *injunction* to stop the man molesting you or any child living with you; an order stopping him from entering the house, or restricting him to a specified part; to an order that he allows you back into the house – if you have been forced out. If you have actually been assaulted by the man, the judge can add a power of arrest to the order he makes, which enables you to turn to the police for help if the violence is repeated, showing the police officer the judge's order. This will enable the man to be arrested and brought before the judge or a county court within twenty-four hours. I must add that the police don't *have* to step in, despite the order; but one hopes that they will do so. You may be able to find a solicitor to help out of office hours (see question 442).

84 Would I be able to use this history of violence as grounds for divorce? Or to start the divorce within the three years?

A. Violence is something which is almost certainly unreason-

42

able behaviour. To start off within the three years you have to show that you have suffered *exceptional hardship* or that your spouse has been guilty of *exceptional depravity*. This is difficult to explain, because the approach to it varies so much from court to court; and what is hardship or depravity to one person may be perfectly normal to someone else. Judges are human and have their own views, although, of course, they will try to understand how the person feels about the treatment to which he/she has been subjected. It is always worth taking legal advice about it, though there is no guarantee that you will be able to do anything positive to get out of your marriage ahead of time.

85 Earlier you stated that one had to have lived in England for at least a year to be able to take divorce proceedings. Why is this?

A. The reason for the qualifying period is that the courts of a country can only deal with divorce for people who are *domiciled* in that country. To this principle there are, inevitably, exceptions; there are a substantial number of people living in England and Wales who are *not* domiciled here. Because there would be considerable hardship to many of them if they could not obtain a divorce here the rules have been eroded. (For instance, according to the rules, a Scot would be prevented from taking divorce proceedings in England – even though he had lived here for years.) So, in most cases, a person who has been resident here for at least twelve months can go to the court like someone who was born here.

86 I was born in England and married here; then my husband – who was born in Scotland – and family went with me to South Australia where we intended to settle. The trip was an assisted emigration. After several years there, I left my husband and lived in different places in Asia before meeting a Belgian and eventually returning to Holland to live. My Belgian and I have

two children, one born in India, the other in Switzerland. He and I want to marry, but I am not free to do so. How can I get a divorce?

A. This is the sort of question which student lawyers relish. Your *domicile of origin* (the one you got when you were born) was England and Wales. When you married, which was before 1974, you, as a wife, automatically took on your husband's domicile of origin – which was Scotland; this is called a *dependent domicile*. When you emigrated to South Australia, your intention was to settle for the rest of your lives; your husband is still there. So he changed his domicile to South Australia when you went there, and yours automatically changed too. And *that* is where you are still domiciled. Your world trip doesn't alter that. So, unless there is some rule in Holland which enables you to take divorce proceedings without being domiciled there, the only place where you can get divorced is South Australia; and I do not know what the grounds for divorce are there. There are just two other possibilities. One is that in the United Kingdom the law on a woman's dependent domicile has been changed. You might be able to claim that you had abandoned your domicile in South Australia and had re-adopted that in England. But residence is a factor in showing that this is so, and living in Holland would make it hard. The second idea is for you to come back to England and live here for a year; then you can take divorce proceedings on the ground of five years separation.

87 How does a marriage get annulled?

A. An application by petition for a *nullity* decree can be made at any time on the grounds that the marriage has not been consummated through incapacity or refusal; within three years, on the grounds that there was no valid consent to the marriage; that one party was mentally ill, or was suffering from venereal disease, or was pregnant by someone other than the applicant.

88 Are some marriages void?

A. Yes. A bigamous marriage; one where the parties are too closely related; where one party is under age – these, among others, are void; that means that there is no marriage. But a decree of nullity does not prevent a court making orders relating to maintenance, property, and, of course, any children.

89 Is there any way in which – as a grandparent – I can see my grandchildren? My daughter and her husband are separated and they just won't come to see me or even let the children talk to me on the phone.

A. I can give you both good and bad news. First, the good: if there are divorce proceedings, the court can make any order it thinks fit about the custody of a child – and custody includes access. So the judge could make some reference to access to grandparents – though it would be unusual, and would require you being legally advised and represented. Not easy. If you felt the children were in physical or moral danger – or were being neglected, you could apply to make them *wards of court*. In this procedure the judge is asked to hear evidence from all people involved – the parents, grandparents (if they began the case), the children if they are old enough, and welfare officers or social workers, as well as doctors and teachers. Ward of court cases are usually started when one parent believes that the other is leaving the country, or if there is neglect or danger to the way the children are being brought up. The bad news is that it is not easy – and it is expensive, because it has to be started in the High Court. The slightly better news is that a new Act will give limited rights to grandparents – but *only* limited ones. You may apply on your own initiative (rather than waiting for someone else to get the case before the court) for access if either or both of the natural parents are dead; BUT you must be the parent of a dead parent of the child, *not* of the surviving parent. Try and get on terms with your daughter, remembering that she has problems of her own right now.

3

HOUSING

90 What is the point of having a solicitor to act for me when I buy a house?

A. It should give you peace of mind and enable you to concentrate on the problems of getting a mortgage and arranging the move. It also costs you money. The solicitor's task is to make certain that the legal title to the plot of land on which the house stands is correct, that it really does belong to the people who are claiming to be able to sell it, and that they are not bankrupt. He also checks to see that the local planning restrictions which may relate to the house have been followed, as far as extensions or gardens are concerned, that the drains are connected to the mains, and that new roads are not planned within 200 yards of it. He approves the contract and prepares the transfer document and – usually, but not always – the mortgage. Finally he deals with all the financial arrangements necessary to ensure that there is the right money in the right place at the right time. It all sounds simple, and it usually is straightforward. Just once in a while things go wrong, and your solicitor should be able to cope with the problems.

91 What do solicitors charge?

A. It is difficult to say nowadays; there used to be scale charges based on a percentage. While these were said to be unfair, at least they did provide a guide and you knew where you stood at the outset. Now most solicitors will quote a figure for their fees for house purchase and sale, which is usually between $\frac{1}{2}\%$ and 1% of the price – plus a bit.

92 I was horrified to get a bill for hundreds of pounds from my solicitor. I had no idea that it could be so expensive, and I was shocked that he should expect me to pay such huge sums, especially as he simply deducted the money from the sale proceeds and sent me a receipt!

A. Hold on! Before you hit the ceiling let us look at the things which you have to pay when you *buy* a house. You will have to pay *stamp duty* if the house costs more than £15,000; if the title is registered you have to pay *Land Registry* fees; you will have to pay for the searches; you will have to pay any bank charges that the solicitor incurs for transferring your money around the country; you will have to pay his fares and phone and postage charges; and, lastly, you will have to pay his bill and V.A.T. If the building society or insurance company you are borrowing money from use their own solicitor, as they sometimes do, you will have to pay those fees as well. So, the money you pay is not all going into one solicitor's pocket by any means.

93 What is stamp duty and the Land Registry fee?

A. The first is a tax on the transfer of land. The rate over £15,000 is $\frac{1}{2}$%; over £20,000 – 1%; over £25,000 – $1\frac{1}{2}$%; and over £30,000 it is 2%. There is a similar sort of scale for leaseholds, although if there is a heavy annual rent as well as a lump sum payable, the stamp duty can be much higher. And the duty starts at a lower figure too. Illogical and unfair – but that is tax for you. The Land Registry is a government department which indexes all titles to land and issues certificates guaranteeing the title when it is *registered*. Each time land changes hands, a fee based on the price is payable; at present it is £2.50 per £1000 up to £20,000; above that it is £50 for the first £20,000 and thereafter £2.40 per £1000. So that can be quite a hefty sum too. The searches cost £5.75 plus an extra 50p per person buying for a bankruptcy search (see question 120). Bank charges, post, phone calls and fares can be £10 to £20 plus V.A.T. Then at the end is the charge that your solicitor makes. The building society's solicitor's charge is now based on a scale. A mortgage of £12,000 attracts a scale fee of £47 – plus V.A.T.

94 My wife and I are buying a house for £27,000 with a mortgage of £15,000 and a life policy. What sort of cost will we incur?

A. Stamp duty = £405; Land Registry fees = £66.80; searches = £6.75; solicitor's fees for the purchase of the house, say £270; for seeing to the mortgage and life policy, say £50; both plus V.A.T.; the solicitor's postage and phone calls, say £15 plus V.A.T. On top is the valuation fee you pay to the building society for the mortgage (see question 106).

95 How can I find out these costs?

A. Ask your solicitor! He is acting for you and will quite understand your anxiety to know how much money is involved. And make these enquiries before you start; ask one or two firms and see if there is any appreciable difference. Some smaller local firms will charge less than big city firms.

96 What about selling a house? Are the fees the same?

A. There is no stamp duty and the only fee payable to the Land Registry is for a copy of the details on the register. You will have to pay commission to any estate agent you have used (see question 132). The solicitor will charge you a fee which is usually based on the price, and is again between $\frac{1}{2}\%$ and 1 %. If you are paying off a mortgage there may be a fee payable to the solicitor who acts for the building society for the production of the deeds and the issue of a receipt. This may be £15 plus V.A.T.

48

97 You have not commented on the practice of deducting money for fees from the proceeds of sale. Is it in order to do this?

A. Providing everyone knows about it, yes. It is a perfectly sensible way of accounting and saves time and money. But it is a bad practice simply to lop off your fees without telling the client in advance, particularly if there is then an argument about the fees charged. Any prudent solicitor will prefer to have the money in his hand because clients have been known to be less than enthusiastic about paying quite reasonable bills. So most firms will tell you in advance what the costs and *disbursements* will be and ask you to agree to them being deducted.

98 What can I do if I don't agree the solicitors' fees and he won't adjust them?

A. You can do one of two things. First, ask him to obtain a *Remuneration Certificate* from the Law Society – the solicitors' ruling body. To do this, you simply write and ask him to get on with it. He submits his bill and details to The Law Society who ask you to comment on the figures. Then an assessment is made and a Certificate issued which says whether or not they consider the account fair and reasonable. If they think it is too high they state what a fair figure would be. That is usually all you have to pay. Secondly, you can apply to a court for the bill to be assessed by a court official. This takes time, costs money and puts you in jeopardy to pay still more costs if the bill is upheld or only a small amount is deducted.

99 Do these rights extend to the fees I have to pay to the building society's solicitor?

A. You cannot obtain a Remuneration Certificate. So you can only apply to the court for an assessment for any bill

which you have to pay but which is for work done for someone else. This is very hard if you are faced with a heavy bill
from a society's solicitor; the fee will be deducted from the
mortgage advance so that you *have* to pay it as a condition
of getting the mortgage you need to buy the house. If you
challenge the matter vigorously, the building society may
take it up with the solicitor – but don't bank on it. You really
have to grit your teeth and pay.

**100 These searches don't seem to me to tell me anything
useful. After I bought my house it turned out that there was to
be a large housing development in the open fields across the
road. The solicitor never discovered that. And a friend had a
factory built down his road bringing construction lorries and
then heavy traffic. His solicitor didn't tell him about that,
either.**

A. Try and understand what the searches are for. You are
buying a plot of land. Your solicitor is concerned with the
legal ownership of that plot of land *and no other*. The
searches are made in the local authority and cover the
matters I indicated in question 90 plus some others insofar
as they relate to the bit of land you are buying. Not next
door; not across the road; not down the end of the lane.
The plot you are after. No more, no less. (The only exception
is for road building within 200 yards.)

**101 Well, in that case, what can I do to find out about likely
developments in the neighbourhood?**

A. Search against other properties, if you want to. Or, more
effectively, go to the planning department of the local council
and ask them what the planning proposals are. You will
find that most planning officials are extremely helpful – and
will be happy to talk about their plans; after all, you are
making enquiries about their work! But they will be reluc-

tant to commit themselves to a definite 'yes' or 'no' to questions about what is to happen in this field or on that derelict site.

102 What about the house itself; doesn't the solicitor make any enquiries about it and its condition? If not, why not?

A. The solicitor's job is primarily to ensure that the *plot of land* you are buying belongs to the seller. He does ask questions about fences, woodworm guarantees, fixtures and fittings and other matters relating to the use of the land; and he may well ask additional ones about insulation, rewiring, subsidence and whether anything left on the premises – like gas and electric cookers – actually belongs to the seller. But the seller doesn't have to answer them; 'not to the vendor's knowledge' is a legal cliché frequently seen on the replies to these questions. The only point about them is that if the seller *does* answer them and is wrong, then you *may* have a legal claim against him. But the main burden of finding out about the house is on *you*.

103 How do I do this? I don't like to bother the people who are living there.

A. Why on earth not? You are about to pay a large sum of money to buy your dream house. The people selling want your money. But because it's a house and there is someone living in it, you feel awkward. Don't. Go there as often as you want, taking a tape measure. Look through each room, measure up, see that it conforms to the estate agent's blurb. Ask if you can run the taps, flush the lavatory, jump on the floors. No one will object if there is nothing to hide. Ask if you can get into the roof and inspect the cold water tank, the insulation and, indeed, the condition of the roof tiles and slates. Ask about the central heating system. Has it ever packed up; are spares easy to get; has it been regularly maintained? If it is oil-fired, who supplies the fuel and are they reputable and reliable? Ask whether you can see the gas and electricity bills so that you can judge how much it is going to cost you to run the place. It is also quite a good idea to go there on a rainy day, not only to see if you like the place when it's wet, but also to see if puddles form or the gutters leak or damp patches appear in angles and corners.

104 Do I need a surveyor to look at the house for me?

A. This is a personal view; it all depends on the house. If it was built in the last ten or fifteen years, then it *ought* not to need a survey, because worm and damp should not happen in modern houses, and there should not be structural faults. That is not to say they do not exist in recently built places; but they *should* not. For an older house a surveyor may well be a good idea, because he may spot the expensive problems – worm, damp, rot, faults and subsidence, as well as leaky tanks – and so enable you either to abandon the house or haggle with the seller. Remember that the building society will arrange for a *valuation* to be done. This is often called a *survey* – but it isn't that. It is a *valuation* carried out because the law says that it must be done to ensure that the society's money is protected. In the course of that valuation, the surveyor may well spot things which might affect the mortgage, like suspect wiring (a fire hazard), damp, rot, worm or subsidence. These matters may make the society not lend, or retain some of the money until specified work has been done, or withhold all of it until other work has been done. If you want a surveyor of your own to go over the house, it might be an idea to ask the building society for the name of their man, so that you can instruct him to do a full structural survey for you at the same time as he does his valuation. This will save some time, and, with luck, some money too.

105 At what stage ought I to find out about a mortgage?

A. That should be practically the first thing you do. I am still amazed that people get fairly well advanced in the buying game without having given any thought to the mortgage. Especially nowadays, when the availability of funds varies so much, you would do well to have been a regular saver with a society (or with several) and made enquiries about their policy towards mortgage requests. Some societies prefer first-time buyers, especially as there is now a government scheme for first-timers which is geared to regular saving called *Homeloan*. And don't fall into the trap of thinking that because you already have a mortgage on your present house, you will automatically be able to get one for your next buy. Most times you can – but there is *no* guarantee.

106 What is the procedure for getting a mortgage?

A. This is not really a legal question. You apply to the building society (or insurance company) of your choice; you may also try the local authority. They take details of your income, etc., – and sometimes, not always, that of your partner. When you find a house, the society will arrange for the *valuation* to be done – and you will have to pay a fee for this based on the value of the house, NOT on the size of the mortgage you want. Once the valuation has been done, the society will make a written *offer*, which is part of a legally binding contract. You must *accept* this in writing and send the appropriate form back to the society, which then earmarks the cash and instructs its solicitor. It is helpful if you keep a copy of the mortgage offer and let your solicitor see it, especially if it contains conditions. You may want to opt for an *optional mortgage*.

107 My mortgage offer contained conditions about my having to put on a new roof and get a woodworm specialist report. I got estimates for the building work and for woodworm treatment, but the society said that they would withhold half the mortgage until the work was done. This seems crazy to me, since without the mortgage I can't buy the house. Isn't there any way round this?

A. Your society is making its offer subject to a *retention*. Get a *bridging loan* from your bank. If you haven't got a bank account, your solicitor will be able to give you an introduction to at least one of the main banks in your town. Bridging loans are usually made available to you on production of a mortgage offer and confirmation from your solicitor that the purchase is proceeding normally. You can then obtain the rest of the money to enable you to buy the house and get the work done. Once it has been finished and the society's valuer is happy, the balance of the money retained will be released to you or to your solicitor, and the bank can be paid off.

108 Won't this bridging loan cost me money?

A. Yes, of course. You will have to pay interest and also an initial *commitment fee* – a charge by the bank for providing the facility. But if you want the house, this is the way you have to go to finance it. The commitment fee varies from bank to bank and also depends on your rating with the bank as a customer. The manager has a wide discretion as to what he charges you. You can get tax relief on the interest you pay on this bridging loan.

109 A lot of the letters being written by the solicitors are marked *subject to contract*. What does this mean?

A. Until contracts are exchanged (see question 113) there is no binding arrangement between you and the person selling the house. So each side can back out, increase the price or try to get it reduced. And to be enforced anyway, a contract for the sale of land must be in writing. Using the formula 'subject to contract' ensures that everyone knows that there is not a binding deal and protects the right of either side to withdraw.

54

110 The estate agent acting for me insisted that I paid a deposit to him to make sure I got the house. Can he do this, and does paying a deposit mean that I am better off than anyone else who is after the house?

A. No, it does not. There is NO legal deal until you have exchanged contracts. Paying money to an estate agent may give the impression to the seller that you are really in earnest, but it is no guarantee that the house will be yours. And you might just consider whether the estate agent belongs to a professional association which has a scheme to protect people who have paid money to their members. There have been notorious examples of agents taking deposits from several buyers and then disappearing with the cash. Most reputable agents belong to a body which will compensate you if the agent makes off with the deposit. It is more normal to pay a small preliminary deposit to the agent and then pay the balance of the deposit (see question 111) to the seller's solicitor on exchange of contracts. A final point; the estate agent will almost certainly NOT be acting for you but for the *seller*. Only if you make a special arrangement for an agent to find you a house will he be your agent too.

111 My solicitor tells me that when contracts are exchanged I will have to pay 10% of the price as a deposit. I don't understand this, as I am getting a 95% mortgage, and I don't have access to much cash anyway.

A. He is quite right to warn you about the deposit. Lots of people seem to think that the deposit is just a formality and doesn't actually have to be paid. Not so. You have to be able to put the money on the table. This may well mean a *bridging loan* again. You can also ask your solicitor to enquire if the seller will agree to a smaller deposit; many people will happily agree to this. But you do have to be able to pay it, make no mistake about that.

112 When does one exchange contracts?

A. As soon as you are satisfied that the house is sound (or is what you want) and you have had a written mortgage offer. You can do it sooner, of course, but as you are then committed to buy, it may be risky to exchange contracts without certain confirmation that the mortgage will come through.

113 What happens? Do all the solicitors meet up or do they send contracts by post?

A. In theory – and, indeed, with some solicitors, in practice – one does actually meet and hand over each part of the contract signed by the seller and the buyer respectively. More often, it's done by post. One trouble is that there is often a *chain* of similar transactions on which the sale of the house you are buying may depend, so contracts can't be exchanged on one until all the others are ready.

114 When the solicitors have exchanged, is the deal legally binding? What happens if I change my mind or can't go ahead because of personal reasons or lack of money?

A. Tough; you will almost certainly lose the deposit. That's why you pay it. As soon as contracts are exchanged, there is a binding and enforceable legal relationship between you. The seller cannot put the price up or decide not to sell it to you; you cannot change your mind or call it off. Or if either of you does, the other can get legal advice, and – in the extreme – go to court about it.

115 The contract on my purchase says that completion will be four weeks after exchange. What is meant by completion, and why does it take so long?

A. Last part first; the delay is normal for several reasons. First, you have got to do all the legal things like checking on the title, getting bankruptcy searches done, and, of course, getting hold of the money. And arranging for meter reading, removal firms, new schools, etc., all takes time. The *chain* situation can cause its own delays too. *Completion* is the moment when the seller's solicitor and yours (and the building society's solicitor, if they have their own) will meet to receive the title deeds and hand over the money. It may not sound very much, and often takes only a few minutes – but the deeds and documents are of crucial importance because they are the evidence of the title to the plot you are buying, and no one will part with them until they see the colour of your money – and the right amount too.

116 Is it possible for the process to be speeded up?

A. Certainly; if you have a handful (or sackful) of pound notes and want to cut through the delays, any competent solicitor should be able to do the necessary work in hours, or in a few days at the most. Co-operation from all sides including yourself is vital, of course.

117 Several times you have mentioned registered land. What is this, and what is unregistered land, if that is what it is called?

A. One day every bit of land in the country will be registered at the *Land Registry*. At present, large chunks are registered – especially in towns. Details of all land in a particular area are indexed at a district Land Registry to which application has to be made when a transfer takes place. When land is first registered full details of the land – measurements, rights of way, restrictions and *covenants*, as well as the name of the existing owner, and any mortgage he may have, are noted on an individual file, and particulars of the previous ownership for at least the past fifteen years (and often very much longer than that) are produced. The Land Registry then checks all this information and issues a certificate for that particular plot of land and shows it on a plan. Each title has its own number which it always keeps. Once registered, the title to the land is guaranteed by the state, and the owner shown on the register is presumed to be rightly there. Transfer of registered land is straightforward because the seller says, in effect, 'Here is what the Land Registry says about me and my bit of land. Unless I am a fraud or bankrupt, you must accept this and are protected', except for a few matters which your solicitor will always investigate, called *overriding interests*.

118 And unregistered land?

A. All land that is not *registered*, you will be astounded to learn, is *unregistered*! There the solicitor's task is trickier, because he has to be satisfied that the deeds show a correct succession of owners, that the person selling is the true owner, and that the land actually belongs to him. For houses in streets, there is generally no problem; but when farm-land is involved there can be all sorts of oddities. I recently saw a title deed referring to a field which had been in the same family for over 200 years, and there was no document which showed just how they had acquired it. Until the sale to my client there had been no dealings with it, although there were all sorts of rights affecting the land. It wasn't an easy thing to cope with at all, and required a lot of research.

119 I want to buy the house jointly with my wife – in both our names, that is. I assume this will not cause any problem?

A. Providing you get the right sort of joint ownership, no problem at all. There are two ways of holding a house (or other things, like money) jointly. The first is called *joint-tenancy*. Here two or more people will hold the house jointly so that when one dies his or her share passes automatically to the survivor. The other is called *tenancy-in-common*. In this case two or more people hold the house jointly in such a way that when ones dies his or her share forms part of the estate and does NOT pass automatically to the survivors. There can be advantages from a Capital Transfer Tax angle to tenancy-in-common (see question 391).

120 You have kept mentioning *bankruptcy* throughout this section; why?

A. Because a person who is bankrupt cannot own a house. So it is vital to know if the seller is bankrupt. If he is, he cannot sell and cannot receive the money. To hand over the money without checking on the seller's bankruptcy would be negligence by your solicitor. When the title is registered, notice of bankruptcy automatically appears on the Land Register. But when it is unregistered the search has to be made against all owners in the immediate past. The building society will also want to know if *you* are bankrupt, because if you are they will not lend you the money since you could not own a house. So the solicitor will do a *bankruptcy search* on you.

121 My house is semi-detached, and some of my gutters overhang next door's garden. I want to get at them to clean them out and to paint the outside of my house. My neighbour and I don't get on – to put it mildly. Have I a right to go on his land and to put a ladder up? He says I don't, and that he will 'get me' if I try to do so.

A. You do not have a right to enter anyone else's land unless they invite you to or give you a *licence* to do so. So you would be breaking the civil law if you did go on to your neighbour's land by trespassing. And he can sue you for damages, if he feels that strongly about it. What a court would award him is another matter; little or nothing I expect. There is just a chance that the deeds of your house give you some right of access for things like cleaning gutters or painting, so it would be worth checking that.

122 How can tradesmen come into my garden if they are trespassing?

A. They are not; you give them an *implied licence* – that is, by saying nothing to indicate that you don't want them there, you tacitly agree to postmen, milkmen, paper boys, and so on coming on to your land. But if you put up a sign saying 'no hawkers' you are saying that you do not want itinerant salesmen to knock on your door, and if they do so they are trespassing.

123 The people next door never do anything to their garden, and it's a mess. My husband and I like to keep our place looking smart and grow flowers in the summer. Weeds come through from next door. Can't they be made to do something about it?

A. The 'Compulsory Digging Act,' you mean! Seriously, there is very little you can do if gentle persuasion doesn't work. The old saying about an Englishman's castle is true; you can do what you like on your own land – so long as it is not against planning laws, or in contravention of the law of nuisance. And simply letting seeds and weeds blow about (unless there is a local council order in force) is not a *legal* nuisance however much it may be one to you.

124 Does this ruling apply to maintaining a house? The place next door is in a frightful state of disrepair, and I can't trace the owner to try and get him to do something about it. It is badly affecting the value of our house. What can I do? Can I get the owner's name from the Land Registry?

A. Last point first – no; details of land registration are secret. You can only find out if you have the owner's permission to inspect the register. You could try the Rating Department who may have a name of a person listed for rates. But they may be chary about telling you. As to the main question – there is little you can do directly. If the house is dangerous there is power for the local council to take action to safeguard passers-by who might be hit on the head by falling slates, etc. And the council could take action to make the house habitable, or even, if it really wanted to, apply to buy it compulsorily.

125 When we bought our house we did have a surveyor who reported that it was in good repair. There was no mention of dry rot, although we had asked him to check all the important features. It now turns out, six months after we moved in, that there is extensive dry rot in the underfloor cavities. What can I do? The surveyor seems to think it isn't anything to do with him.

A. The first question is what the surveyor should have discovered when he went round the house. If the seller had wall-to-wall carpets or hardboarded floors it might well have been physically impossible, short of ripping holes in the floor covering, to see underneath. Or the seller may have refused to allow an examination. In such a case, the surveyor would not be liable because he could not have looked even if he had wanted to. (He should have told you, of course.) In the event that the floors were exposed to view, what then? Was it possible to get underneath without doing any damage or causing problems to the seller? It is not always easy to find floorboards readily liftable – especially in an older house where they may be tongued and grooved. So the surveyor may have tried but failed for reasons beyond his control. Only if he could have looked, but didn't; or if he could have gone into a cellar, say, and noticed, is there any likelihood of blame. So you need evidence (see question 401) before you can take any action.

126 Who should arrange the insurance on a house, and when does it start to be effective?

A. Normally if you buy a house with a mortgage; the building society or insurance company will protect themselves (and you) by arranging cover against loss by fire and other perils. And with rampant inflation, they will keep the cover up to a realistic figure. It is very easy to under-insure, and there are financial risks if you allow that to happen. When the mortgage is paid off, it will be up to you to make your own insurance arrangements. Insurance is effected at the moment that contracts are exchanged – before you take possession, that is, because you have an insurable interest in the house. This is really a form of double cover, because the seller will almost certainly be insured – but it is worthwhile being absolutely sure.

127 What does the insurance policy cover?

A. The terms vary from company to company. A typical one will cover loss or damage to the house caused by fire, explosion, lightning, riot, civil commotion, aircraft, storm and flood, theft, burst tanks and pipes, being hit by a vehicle, breakage of TV aerials, leaking oil from tank or boiler, subsidence, criminal damage, falling trees. The policy may also cover loss of rent, breakage of basins, lavatories and glass, and your liability for claims made against you for injury or damage to people or property from, for example, slates falling from the roof.

128 I imagine that there are exclusions to these terms?

A. Of course; it wouldn't be an insurance policy if it didn't have them! Exterior damage by frost is excluded, as is subsidence to paths, walls and fences unless the house is also affected at the same time. And theft and malicious damage cover are excluded when the house is empty for more than a month (so watch out if you go on a cruise). It is important to read the insurance policy – or, if it is arranged by a building society – to obtain details from the society of the main terms of cover.

129 I am going to buy a new house, and I am told by the building firm that there is a guarantee with the house and that it is covered by the National House-Building Council. What is this all about, and just what do I get?

A. The National House-Building Council (N.H.B.C.) maintains a register of house builders who have passed their vetting system and are thought to be professionally skilled craftsmen. To participate in the scheme the builder must also agree to provide a two-year warranty against defects, in the house and its major fittings (although central heating and electrical moving parts are only covered for one year). From the third to the tenth year, the N.H.B.C. arranges insurance cover against damage due to major defects in the load-bearing structure only. Because of inflation, there is provision for some inflation-proofing for an additional premium payable by you or the builder when you buy.

130 How does the scheme work, and how does one make a claim under the guarantee?

A. I think the word 'guarantee' is misleading. The N.H.B.C. scheme is designed to impose standards on builders and then enable house owners who suffer damage to have some recompense in limited circumstances. Remember that apart from the inflation-proofing premium (at present £20) you don't pay for this N.H.B.C. scheme, at least not directly. The two-year part is a legal agreement in which the builder undertakes to put right, at his own expense, defects arising from his own failure to comply with the N.H.B.C.'s standards of work and materials. Normal wear and tear and shrinkage are excluded. You claim by getting in touch *in writing* with the builder. You have NO claim against the

63

N.H.B.C. in the first two years – unless the builder has gone into liquidation or bankruptcy. Thereafter you still have a claim, initially against the builder for all defects caused by his bad workmanship; in addition, you have a claim on the insurance arranged by N.H.B.C. if there is damage due to major defects in the load-bearing structure. Excluded are things like defects caused by the negligence of someone other than the builder – wet rot, leaking roofs, defective central heating, external items, damp penetration, unreasonable decay, defects which a second purchaser ought to have seen before he bought. You are still liable for these and other ordinary repairs – unless you can get the builder to do anything for you, or you are prepared to sue him.

131 I don't know whether or not to use an estate agent to sell my house. What do you think?

A. An estate agent can be very useful in arranging and dealing with the sale of a house, especially if you live in an isolated area. If you live in a street in a town you may do as well by getting a 'for sale' board painted and putting it up yourself. Agents will probably have a better idea of the asking price you should expect to get – though this isn't always the case. It is really like the answer to the question about using a solicitor. By employing an expert, you hand over the hassle and the time-consuming worry and drudgery. But you will pay for it. Most estate agents gear their fees to the price of the house rather than the time spent or work done. It is said that the fees charged even out over the house-selling public as a whole. Sometimes the house is sold on the first day, at other times it takes months, and a great deal of work. Charging a level fee is said to be fair on a 'swings and roundabouts' basis. And the client knows exactly how much he will have to pay at the outset. It could be, though, that the same public would rather pay a fair price for the work *actually* done. With the government investigation into estate agents' fees and charging methods, a change may be made.

132 How do the agents assess their fees?

A. Some charge a flat percentage commission, anything from 1% or 1½% up to 3% – and something even higher for low-priced property. Others charge a lower percentage, say 1½%, but expect you to pay the advertising costs. Others still will accept a lowish commission on condition that they have the sole right to deal with the house. Ask for full details before you commit yourself.

133 Can you explain about sole selling rights and sole agency?

A. Yes. *Sole agency* is when you employ one estate agent to try and sell your house and agree that you will not use any other estate agent. The one you choose then has a *sole agency* and can prevent you from employing another agent, by legal action if necessary; or he can claim his fee from you if you do use another agent. *Sole selling rights* means something even more restrictive. You literally give the agent the sole right to sell the house – you cannot even sell it privately yourself. Often you are asked to sign a document by the estate agent. It is important to read and understand its legal effect, because you may be agreeing to sole agency or sole selling rights.

134 I put my house on the market through an estate agent; a buyer was found, and the sale seemed to be going well. Contracts were exchanged, and then the buyer couldn't go through with the purchase for personal reasons. So the deposit was repaid and the house put back on the market through a different agent. I was amazed to get a bill for the full 2% commission from the first agent. Surely I don't have to pay this?

A. The fee which an estate agent charges is in fact a commission which arises when there is a concluded arrangement between you and a buyer. So once contracts have been exchanged, the deal is on; and the event which determines whether the agent has done his job has take place. So he is entitled to his fee.

135 Shouldn't the buyer who changed his mind have paid it?

A. Yes, he should – but not directly. You say you repaid the deposit. I am bound to say I don't know why you did this. The whole point about a deposit is that if the buyer is unable to go through with the purchase, he will *forfeit* the deposit. Lose it, that means. And it is from the forfeited deposit that you pay the agent's commission and the fees which your solicitor will charge. So your kindness in repaying the money was a little misplaced.

136 I am finding it very difficult to pay all the bills and the mortgage. As there are a couple of spare rooms, I was thinking of getting some students or paying guests in to share the cost. Is there anything to stop me doing this?

A. Yes, the mortgage. You will find that many building societies require you to sign an undertaking not to let the premises or to sublet or share. This is not just to be mean; it is because of the great difficulty which they could face if they wanted to get possession and sell if you stopped paying – or defaulted on – the mortgage instalments. So it is very important that you keep your side of that bargain.

137 I found a house which I liked, and went to a solicitor who did all that was necessary, so I thought. I signed the contract and gathered that I would be able to move in on a day about four weeks later. So, I arranged to give up my flat, booked a lorry to move my gear, and duly turned up at the house on the appointed morning. There I found the seller still happily in residence. When I asked what was going on, he said that he

had not exchanged contracts, and that he was still waiting for his new house to become available. How can this happen?

A. Because, I am afraid, you have failed to grasp what was going on, to find out from your solicitor the state of play, and have misunderstood basic steps. Lots of people fall into the same trap of believing that conveyancing is dead easy. *Signing* a contract is NOT the same thing as *exchanging* contracts. You sign it a few days in advance (weeks before, sometimes), so that your solicitor has it available to exchange when the magic moment arrives (see question 112). But until exchange takes place there is NO guarantee whatever that you will actually buy the place. So never move until you know for certain that contracts have been exchanged; tell your solicitor to let you know – in writing if you like – that this step has been taken; or make sure that he phones you to say that all is well. In other words, trust him to do his job – but take nothing for granted.

138 At what stage of the house-hunting saga should I first approach a solicitor?

A. As soon as you have got a mortgage lined up and have found a house which you want to buy and on which the building society will lend money.

139 I don't know a solicitor. The estate agent, who almost got me the mortgage, told me that I should use one which he recommended. When I said that I might like to shop around, he told me that if I wanted the mortgage I should do as he said. He also said that it was a condition of the building society that I used this solicitor.

A. First, any reputable building society will not permit its branch managers to make such conditions. So, you should tell the Chief General Manager of the Society: secondly, it is a breach of the Solicitors Practice Rules for this sort of arrangement to be made, and the solicitor (if he was a party to it) would be liable to disciplinary action by The Law Society. Thirdly, the agent has no right to lay down what solicitor you instruct. You should have complete freedom of choice. If you had asked him for a recommendation, on the other hand, there would be no reason why he shouldn't make one. That is how much business is done, and there is nothing wrong with it in principle. You can find solicitors by looking in the Law List or the Legal Aid Referral List, asking at any local advice centre, consulting the Yellow Pages or your bank, or best of all by asking friends, as they will be unlikely to recommend someone unless they were satisfied with the service they got.

140 Why can't the seller and buyer use the same solicitor? Wouldn't this save time and money?

A. It might save a bit of time; it would save some money because the work would not be duplicated. But it is not done because The Law Society's rules don't allow it – except in very rare cases. It is because a conflict of interest might arise between the seller and the purchaser. I am sure you can see that this might put the solicitor in a very difficult position; he would probably have to stop acting for both people, costs would have been incurred unnecessarily, and everyone would be upset. So, it is said to be in the general public interest for the two parties to use different solicitors.

141 How long after selling a house should I get my money? My house sale was completed over two months ago, but although I ring the solicitor up he tells me that he hasn't got round to dealing with it yet. Is there a specified time?

A. In my view, your solicitor is negligent. There is no good reason why he should not have sent you the money due to you – if not the same day as completion – within a couple of days. By not doing so, he has failed in his professional obligation to you – and you have a cast iron case against him for the interest on the money from completion to payment.

142 Assuming I own my house, with a mortgage, am I secure? I mean, can I ever be evicted?

A. The Rent Acts do not apply to you because you are an owner-occupier; so you can't be evicted by anyone – *except* the building society. If you stop paying the mortgage and get into arrears, the building society is entitled to take court action to obtain possession of the house. And if they can show that you have no intention or ability to pay the arrears, and their loan is at risk, they will get an order for possession. Often this may be held in abeyance if you try to pay off what is due; but it can be put into effect. If this happens you can be made to leave.

143 Can the building society sell the house? If they do, what happens to the money?

A. Yes, they can sell – though they are expected to get the best available price for the house. They repay the loan, the arrears, any second mortgage, the legal costs, and the expenses of the sale. What is left, if anything, is payable to you. If there is a shortfall, you will be expected to repay it in the same way as any other debt.

144 I have taken out a second mortgage to pay for work to be done to the house. This loan was from a banking company. The interest rate seemed reasonable, but turns out to be high. I got into arrears, and now they have threatened to take possession. What can I do to stop this happening?

A. There are a number of ways in which you may be able to avert the worst. Ask your building society if it can lend you enough money to pay off this second mortgage and all the arrears (the rate of interest will be lower); consider asking the court to rule whether the second loan is an *extortionate credit bargain* (see question 409); ask your solicitor to find out what reduction the banking company would accept for immediate repayment of the debt – because this will show you what to aim for in your search for alternative funds; see your own bank manager and find out if he can help. Above all, tell the building society straight away so that they know what is going on. It is unlikely that the society will want the house to be sold if there is any way of saving the situation. But, if all things fail, the second *mortgagee* can obtain a possession order and sell the house.

4

SHOPPING

145 What are all these shopping rights that one hears so much about, and how valuable are they when one has a problem with goods which turn out to be defective?

A. Let me try and put the thing into its legal perspective. Such rights as exist almost all stem from the *contract* which you have with the person who sells you goods. This *contract* is a legally binding arrangement which gives rights and obligations on both sides. So, your redress, if any, is against the shop which sold you the goods, or the tradesman who supplied them while doing work for you. Generally, you have NO legal claim against the manufacturer of the goods – because you had no contract with him. You may be able to take some action if you can show that the manufacturer was *negligent* in the way he made the goods, but this is a very difficult thing to prove and is expensive and uncertain. So, if the new bath has a chip in the enamel, or the new kettle doesn't work, or any other new product doesn't do what it is expected to do – then don't think that you have a legal claim against the firm whose name is on the goods; you do not. Go back to the shop which sold it, or the man who fitted it for you.

146 What you are saying seems to be quite contrary to common sense. Manufacturers give guarantees about their products, and the shop will be much more likely to tell me to 'take it up under guarantee'. Can you reconcile this apparent conflict?

71

A. I agree with your first point; a recent survey showed that 55% of people asked thought that manufacturers *were* at present liable to people who are injured by defective products. And the whole idea of *producer responsibility* increases this view. The widespread use of 'guarantees' (see question 208) as a sales gimmick also confuses shoppers and traders alike. But the basic liability is with the seller of goods; it may seem illogical and the law may need to be changed. Until it is, that is how it stands.

147 Can you explain what shopping rights are, then?

A. Put as simply as possible, a shopper is entitled to be sold goods which are of a reasonable quality and fit for the purpose for which he wants them. If the goods do not comply because there is an *inherent* defect, the shopper has the right to look to the trader who sold them for compensation.

148 I am a trader running a small shop. People keep asking – indeed demanding – to buy things which I have in the window on display. I don't want to mess about with my window arrangements because they take a lot of time. Am I obliged to do so?

A. You do not have to sell anything to anyone (providing you don't discriminate on grounds of race or colour). You don't even have to have people in your shop! And you can't be required to sell any particular item. Displaying goods in the window or in the shop is what lawyers call an *invitation to treat*, and is simply an indication to the world that you deal in things like them. So, a shopper can ask to buy 'the one in the window', but you can quite legally refuse. There is no way in which you can be made to sell.

149 How does one make a contract?

A. By two people agreeing to do business. For there to be a binding and enforceable contract for the sale of goods there must be an *offer* by one side which is unconditionally *accepted* by the other. In normal shopping the *offer* comes from the consumer nearly every time; only if the trader says, 'Do you want to buy this?', and shoves some desirable thing at you, will he be making the offer. There are other exceptions, of course; what area of law would be complete without them? But this is the basic situation; plus, of course, the existence of a *price*.

150 I thought a contract had to be in writing and signed over a sixpenny stamp to be legal?

A. That dates you! A contract can be made in three ways – in writing, by word of mouth and by conduct. Apart from *hire-purchase* and *credit sale* agreements, which have to be in writing, there is nothing significant about a contract for the sale of goods not being in writing. Stamp duty on contracts was abolished years ago – and only related to contracts for the sale of land anyway! (see also question 395).

151 Can you give examples of the way in which a contract can be made by these different methods?

A. Certainly. Take writing first. For example, mail order – you fill in a coupon and send it off to the company *offering* to buy the goods that they have in their advert or catalogue. The company can *accept* by sending an acknowledgement, or *reject* because they have run out of the goods. The onus is on the company to decide what it wants to do about your offer. Or buying a new car; you may well indulge in a lot of sales talk before you finally decide on which one you want. But the garage will then reduce the chat into writing on a sales invoice, which will probably contain small print about the details like price, delivery, quality, etc. And contracts in writing are very often made by traders dealing with other traders, although you can sometimes have an interesting discussion as to whose terms you are trading on.

152 Can what is said overrule the written contract?

A. Generally, no. The exception is for statements which the trader makes prior to the contract being made, upon which you rely, but which turn out to be wrong. If you would not have entered into the deal but for the statements, you may have a claim despite what is in writing. Other than that, you are presumed to have read and understood any contract which you sign – even though you may have done neither. Many people realize in the cold light of dawn that they want to change their minds only to find that there is small print which prevents them from doing so. So, the golden rule about written contracts is: never sign anything you don't understand.

153 What about contracts made by word of mouth?

A. These are the most common: 'will you sell me this one?'; 'a pint of bitter, please'; 'evening paper, please'; 'a pound of sprouts'; you can think of a thousand examples, I am sure. The shopper is *offering* to buy each time; the trader can *accept* or *reject*.

154 I have often found that people deny what was said when I take things back to shops, and say it is just my word against theirs. If what you say about making a contract is right, the words used can be crucial. How do you prove it later?

A. I agree that words can be very important. Proving what took place is a matter of *evidence* (see questions 401/2), but the fact that the whole thing was arranged by word of mouth in no way alters the legality of the contract or does you out of your rights.

155 I suppose that a slot machine is an example of a contract being made by conduct. How do the 'offer' and 'acceptance' work here?

74

A. The owner of the machine holds it out as being able to accept your money. So, he is *offering* to sell you a packet of cigarettes, or a ticket, or to allow you to use his car park, and you can accept this by sticking your money in the slot. At that second, there comes into being a binding contract; so, if the cigarettes don't materialize, there is a breach of contract by the company which owns the machine. And anything that is printed on the ticket or receipt that you get from the machine must tie in with what was said by the company in any notice stuck on the machine, or relating to its use.

156 Is this the only type of offer by conduct?

A. No! When you hand over the appropriate coppers in exchange for a paper or magazine; when you do the same in a shop for a tin of beans; or even when you take a trolley full of goods to the checkout in a supermarket – nothing may be said at all. But each time you proffer an article to the sales assistant at the till you are *offering* to buy it, and that *offer* is *accepted* by the buttons being pressed on the till. So, if you buy thirty things in a supermarket, you make thirty contracts. And you can stop at any time by simply stopping taking things out of the trolley.

157 What happens if you haven't got enough money to pay for the things? I was in a shop the other day and this happened. The trader said that he would hold on to the stuff until I got some cash and suggested that if I didn't come back that day, he would put it back into stock.

A. The moment the contract is made ('Will you sell me this tin?' – 'Yes I will' = a contract) the goods become yours (unless the seller says that he retains ownership until he is paid). And, as they are yours, you own them and the trader cannot put them back on the shelf or sell them to anyone else – because they are NOT his. He does have a right to retain physical possession of what have now become your goods because he has a 'lien'. This means a right to hold on to property until payment. But the *lien* is lost if the physical possession of the goods is lost; so, a trader cannot repossess something which has been sold in an attempt to exercise his lien because it is too late. Of course you have to pay for the goods; and it is possible that if they are perishable and you do not offer the money within a reasonable time, the trader can resell them (although he is then selling *your* goods – *not* his).

158 Is this transfer of ownership of any importance in practical terms?

A. Certainly, because it can be very important to know just who does own something; if there is a fire or other damage, for instance, who stands the loss? Also, the transfer of ownership means that the seller has lost his rights over the goods so that he cannot resell (unless perishable goods are involved), nor can he retake possession. Don't forget that a considerable amount of trade is done on the basis of the customer taking the goods home with him and paying for them later, by sending a cheque, or by paying a monthly account, or by making a credit agreement (other than a hire-purchase one, where the ownership does not change hands (see question 181). Or the goods may stay in the shop for the trader to deliver.

159 How can a trader retain ownership?

A. By saying so in the contract, or at the time the contract is made. 'The goods remain our property until they are paid for in full' is a simple form of words a prudent trader may print on his invoices or order forms. Everyone then knows where he stands, and the trader retains rights over the goods which he can enforce without any need to go to court. It is also a sensible thing to do when you sell a car privately because if the buyer's cheque bounces, you can go and take the car because it is *still yours*.

160 I have heard of some way in which a manufacturer may retain ownership, so that the retailer never gets the right to own the goods. Can you explain this?

A. Yes. *Retention of title*, as it is known, is not a new idea. But it has become much more common, especially with foreign sellers of goods and raw materials. The manufacturer (A) will say, in a typical contract, that he will retain title to the goods he has sold until he has been fully paid for everything forming part of that contract. So, if A sells, say, 200 items to a trader (B), who, in turns, sells 90 of them, A still owns the remaining 110. If B goes bust, A can simply take back the 110 items – because they are still his. A is also entitled to be paid for the 90 and can trace the money which B received and take it if he can find it. But B can transfer ownership to the shopper because A supplied B on the understanding that B would be selling to the public. So A has no claim against you for the item you bought and paid for.

161 I am having a long argument with a trader about the price I should pay for some goods which were ordered for me. At the time we made the bargain, the price was £150; it took nearly a year for the goods to materialize, and when they did the price was – so the trader said – £200. I disagreed, and so we argued. Who is right?

A. I wish I knew the answer to that. It all depends. If you did talk about price, and you both knew that £150 was the going rate, then there is a good chance that that was the *agreed price*. If it was, then that is what you must pay. But if there was no agreement about price, you have to pay a *reasonable price*. Now reasonable is a word which lawyers use a great deal and love dearly – because it is like the length of the proverbial piece of string; it means what you want it to mean! What is a *reasonable* price for goods which took so long to be delivered? In an age of inflation, I suppose it could be said that everyone knows that prices are rising all the time and that a *reasonable* purchaser would know this and appreciate that the price will be higher. And so one could use, say, the Index of Retail Prices as a yardstick and see by what amount prices have gone up in the waiting period. It might be £50 – or more, or less. The tedious argument could be avoided quite simply by the trader saying 'the price to be paid is the price ruling at date of delivery'; then there is no uncertainty.

162 Can a child make a contract?

A. Of course; they do it every moment of the day – by buying comics, sweets, bus and train tickets, records, shoes, food . . . you name it. The only oddity about children shopping is that they cannot be forced to pay for something unless it is said to be *necessary* for them to have. There can be a certain amount of argument about just what *is* necessary for a child, but a lot of this argument is likely to be academic because in nearly every case the child will have paid for the goods. Most shops will not make a hire-purchase or credit agreement with a person under eighteen – certainly not without a guarantor (see question 333) – because of some doubts about enforceability. What if the child stops paying? So much depends on the goods sold. A £500 ring might well not be a necessary thing for a seventeen-year-old to buy even if he wants to marry the lucky girl he gives it to. But a motor bike costing £1000 bought by a seventeen-year-old apprentice living in a remote part of the country where there is little or no public transport, so that he can get to work, would almost certainly be regarded as a perfectly proper purchase. So, don't get bogged down in misconceptions about the ability of children to make contracts in the same way as you and me. If you send your child out to buy something for you, on the other hand, the child is acting as your agent, and you are liable to pay for it.

163 I paid a deposit to a shop for some goods. Later I wanted to cancel the contract, because I didn't like them. The shop refused to make any refund to me. Have I a claim?

A. First, let us see just what it was you did pay to the shop. If you saw something and asked the shop to keep it for you until you could come in later and buy it, you may well have been asked to pay a sum of money 'as a deposit'. The payment was *not* a deposit. It was the payment of a sum of money for an option to go in later and make an offer to buy. Almost certainly the trader would take the option payment into account when working out the final price. But, providing you and the shop each fulfilled your respective part of the arrangement, the option would have been worked out. If you went in before the expiry date and the goods had been sold, you would have a good claim for your money back; equally, if you went in too late, the trader would be entitled to keep the money and to have sold the item.

164 If that is not a deposit, what about when I buy goods and pay part of the price prior to them being delivered to me?

A. That is not a deposit either! It is a *part-payment* of the purchase price, so if you go home and break the news of your splendid new acquisition, and your spouse tells you to go back and un-buy it, the shop is not entitled as of right to keep the part-payment. It is entitled to *damages* (see question 209) because of your breach of contract, but the damages may or may not be the same as the amount of money you handed over.

165 What is a deposit?

A. It is a payment in advance which the trader insists on as a condition of doing business with you. In other words, the trader will not sell the goods or allow you to make the contract *unless* you pay a proportion of the price. It is exactly like the deposit you pay on buying a house (see question 111). If you change your mind or cancel the contract, the deposit may be forfeited by the trader. That is why he will have demanded the deposit. The test is: would you have been able to make the contract if you had not paid the money? If the answer is no – then what you paid *is* a deposit. This is common in some sections of retail trade and in other areas like holiday accommodation.

166 The other day I was in a dress shop where there were blouses on a rack priced at £4.99, but when I took one to the sales girl to pay for it, she told me it was £6.99. I pointed to the price label, but she said that it was a mistake. I refused to pay the extra £2, and she refused to sell the blouse. What is the legal situation?

A. The girl was perfectly entitled to refuse to sell it to you. You *offered* to buy at £4.99; she *rejected* that offer and made a *counter-offer* to sell to you at £6.99. You refused to *accept*. So – no contract. The shop was breaking the criminal law, though. The Trade Descriptions Act of 1968 makes it an offence to make a false price indication. So you could notify the Trading Standards Department of your local council, and they might prosecute the shop. Even if the prosecution were successful and the shop convicted, you would still have no right to demand that the blouse be sold to you at £4.99, or at any price.

167 There is a lot of talk about implied terms in contracts; what are these all about, and how can one tell what they are?

A. In every contract for the sale of goods there is *implied* (that means: not expressly stated somewhere in the contract, but automatically included) a condition that the goods will correspond with any description applied to them, will be of merchantable quality (see question 171) and will be fit for their intended use. These things cannot be excluded or avoided in a contract with a private shopper. They are there because the law says so. The last two really are the cornerstone of what has become known as consumer protection, because together they mean that goods must – generally speaking – do what they are meant to and be of a reasonable standard.

168 Is there no way in which the merchantable quality condition can be avoided?

A. Oddly enough, there is. I say oddly because with the legislation to protect the consumer and recent criminal laws, too, one would have thought that the whole thing was watertight. The law says that where a person sells goods in the cause of a business, there will be an implied condition of merchantable quality, *except* in two cases. The first is where there are defects 'specifically drawn to the buyer's attention before the contract is made'. This means what it says; the defect must be identified – so signs simply saying 'seconds' or 'reject stock' or 'sub-standard' or 'shop-soiled' will not help the trader unless whatever caused the reduction to be made is listed and *specifically* pointed out to the potential buyer. The notice or sign will indicate that the goods are not as good as new, but the presence of defects will still make the trader liable. The second exception is where 'the buyer examines the goods before the contract is made as regards defects which that examination ought to reveal'. Again the buyer will have to have examined the goods (or got someone to do it for him), and the inspection made should have shown up what went wrong. For example, you might have a car examined by a skilled mechanic. That is an *examination*; and it ought to reveal things like the adequacy of the steering system, whether the brakes are working and not corroded, and that there is an engine and a wheel at each corner with a legal tyre on it. But it would not discover that there was a defect inside the engine itself. So, if you bought on the strength of the report and then the brakes packed up because of corrosion, the garage could say with justification that your examination ought to have revealed this – so, they are off the hook. But if the big end seized up after a few miles, you would still have a claim despite the examination. The important thing to note about both these exceptions is that, to be effective, they must relate to matters said or done *before the contract* was made. It is no good, for example, a shopkeeper calling after you as you leave the shop with goods, 'They don't work, you know.' Or if you discover a serious fault in a car after you have paid for it, having bought it blind, you are protected.

169 Do these implied terms appear, if that is the right word, in contracts for hire or for work which a tradesman does to my house?

A. Not in quite the same way. The Sale of Goods Act which contains these terms is restricted to sales of goods between traders or with consumers. In the case of hire of a television or a car, for example, there are no laid down terms which will be implied by an Act of Parliament. It would be up to the court in any particular case presented to it, although things like correspondence with description, and fitness for purpose, would very likely be held to be implied. There is an analogy with goods which are supplied by a tradesman in the course of doing work – like building or installation, or the servicing of a car or central heating system, for example (these are known as *work and materials* contracts). Until recently, the tradesman (or the hire company) could – and frequently did – exclude their responsibility for the description, quality or fitness of the goods they dealt in. Since 1978 the law has said that where a consumer hires goods or has them supplied in *work and materials* contracts, any term excluding liability will be of no effect.

170 So I can now claim compensation from a car hire firm if the car doesn't work, or from a garage which has not serviced my own car properly?

A. It is not as simple as that. In each case you will need *evidence* to support your case (see questions 401/2), and you will have to show that there has been a breach of contract. The point about the law is that the trader cannot evade his legal liability; but you *still* have to prove your case. If you do, then he can't hide behind the small print. But if you don't satisfy the court – then you still lose, as you always would have done.

171 Is there any legal definition of 'merchantable quality'? There seems to be little meaning to it, and why 'merchantable' – I am not a trader?

A. There is a definition in the Sale of Goods Act, but it doesn't really help you to understand what the phrase means. Ideally the goods should do what an ordinary, reasonable person would expect them to having regard to the price and the sort of job they were bought for. But it is not certain that a court would hold this to be so in every case. *Merchantable* means *saleable* or *marketable* – and does not relate to a merchant as such.

172 What happens if what I buy doesn't work?

A. Much depends on the nature of the defect. If it is fundamental to the whole thing – so that you cannot use it at all, then you may well have the right to reject the goods, cancel the contract, and claim *damages* (see question 209). If the defect is capable of a speedy repair or adjustment to make it work properly, then you may well have *no* right to reject the goods. The most you could claim would be the cost of the repair or adjustment. Another important factor is the length of time you have owned the goods. Once you have had them for a *reasonable* time – which depends on the facts – you *cannot* reject the goods and cancel the contract; you can *only* claim damages. In a recent case, a lady who bought a secondhand car which didn't go very well waited for six

83

months before formally rejecting it. She was held to have lost the right to do so because she had not done it within reasonable time. So the moral is, the moment you discover something is seriously wrong, go back to the shop, tell them and ask for their help. In very many cases, of course, the shop will want to do whatever is commercially acceptable to both sides. If you do not come to a satisfactory compromise, then you should write a letter immediately, keeping a copy, in which you reject the goods, cancel the contract and demand your money back. The trader would not be able to argue later that you had not rejected in time.

173 Surely that is completely contrary to the guarantee which the manufacturer offers?

A. Well, it may be. But that underlines the uncertain state of the law at present. If you rely on the guarantee, which is a perfectly normal and sensible thing to do (so you think), and spend several months going to and fro and then give up and decide to try and enforce your rights against the trader who sold it to you, you may find him saying that you are 'too late' because more than six months has gone by. What to do about this? Take a case all the way to the Court of Appeal and see how you get on. Then write and tell me! Seriously, I think it is very unsatisfactory that one doesn't know exactly where one stands – both as a consumer and a trader. The uncertainty leads to confusion on both sides of the counter and makes the situation worse than it need be.

174 I am a trader, and people keep bringing back articles which they have bought asking for their money back. Do I have to deal with this sort of demand?

A. One can only claim one's money back if the goods are defective or if the trader has said that refund will be made. So, if a shopper simply changes his mind, the trader is under no obligation at all to take the goods back. If he does, then that is a matter of goodwill, and he can lay down terms on which he will accept them back. Usually these are that the shopper is given a credit note or is allowed to buy something else. If nothing suits the shopper that is his bad luck. Of course, some large stores will give money back in full without question if the goods are in their original wrapper or paper bag. That is again a matter of goodwill, although one could say that if the rule is nationally known and applied, it is a term of the contract so that one could *insist* on a refund.

175 To protect myself, as a trader, I have sign up saying 'no money refunded on goods bought here', although I will, of course, give a replacement for items which I accept as defective. The decision is mine and the shopper has to take it or leave it.

A. See you in court soon. Displaying your notice is a criminal offence which, if you are convicted, makes you liable to a fine of up to £400. So, take it down quickly – and any other notice of similar wording like 'no goods exchanged', 'sale goods not taken back' – any form of words which suggests that the trader will not deal with justifiable complaints, or which puts a shopper off pursuing such complaints, is caught by the criminal law. The fact that you would help with what you regard as a proper complaint doesn't help you get out of this crime.

176 Can I insist on my customers producing a receipt before I deal with their complaints? I sell records, and it is possible for someone to buy at a discount shop (or steal them) and then bring them to me, saying they are defective and demanding their money back.

A. You are perfectly entitled to expect a complainant to produce evidence in support of his claim; and to prove that he bought the goods from you. But this is proved by the customer saying that he did and, if he takes it to the limit, by going into the witness box and telling the judge about it on oath. If you don't believe that you sold the record, or that the record *is* defective, you can simply and politely say 'I am sorry, I don't believe you'. If the customer feels that he is right, he can sue you – and if the judge believes him he will win and you will lose. But if he did steal the record or buy it elsewhere, he is unlikely go anywhere near a court or sue you.

177 That is all very well, but I will have a row in the shop and that upsets other potential customers. It is easier to pay up.

A. I think that is a very shortsighted view. First, you don't have to have a slanging match in the shop. Have a good, clearly laid down complaints machinery which the staff know and follow. If the shopper becomes difficult, take him to an office out of the way and try and discuss the matter rationally. Of course, he may tell his friends about his experience in your shop and they may not buy from you. But if the chap *is* a troublemaker, do you want customers like that anyway?

178 It is all very well to say that; I still want evidence of payment, and I have a notice on my shop tills saying 'retain your receipt – no refund without proof of purchase'.

A. Again I believe that this notice infringes the criminal law. It is capable of being read as meaning that you will not deal with genuine complaints unless a receipt is produced.This may put a person off. If he is likely to be put off – then the law is broken. I can see precisely why you are concerned; but I think you are going about looking after your interests in the wrong way. If you must have a notice, why not say something like 'it helps us both if you keep your receipt'?

179 Recently I was amazed to be asked by one of my customers – who was applying for a hire-purchase agreement –

whether I had used a credit reference agency. I told him to mind his own business, but he then sent me a letter demanding to know. What right has he to enquire how I run my business?

A. Every right – to know about himself. The law was changed in 1976 to enable people to have some right to know what information about them was held by credit reference agencies – companies which store facts about credit ratings. A consumer now has the right within twenty-eight days to ask – in writing – any trader to whom he has applied for goods or services on credit for the name and address of any agency consulted. And he can write direct to an agency off his own bat. The trader must tell him the name of any agency consulted if he did consult. But he does not have to disclose an enquiry from a bank or a protection association of which he is a member – because these bodies are not credit reference agencies.

180 What can I do as a customer?

A. Assuming the trader did consult about you, he must tell you the name and address of the agency. Then you can write off to the agency with a fee of 25p asking for a copy of the file they have on you. They must send this to you, and you can read what is said. If you disagree with anything, you can write and ask for it to be corrected; if you and the agency are unable to agree, there is an appeal to the Office of Fair Trading for help in resolving the difficulties. For a trader to refuse to disclose the name and address of the agency and for the agency to fail to respond to a request for details of the file are criminal offences.

181 Do the rights which you have been describing in general apply to hire-purchase? I recently bought a car on h.p. and there are several things seriously wrong with it. The garage isn't interested and I don't know what to do next. Shall I just stop paying the h.p. instalments?

A. NO! Don't ever just *stop paying*. To do so will inevitably brand you as a defaulter, however justified you may be, and once labelled that way life will be increasingly difficult if you want credit again. In a typical case, the way hire-purchase works is this: you find goods and want to buy them but don't have the cash. The trader will agree to a *hire-purchase* agreement, providing the status enquiries which are made show you to be credit worthy. He then presents you with a form to sign. The trader sells the goods to a finance company, which in turn *hires* them to you (hence *hire-purchase*), in return for which you pay instalments for an agreed period. At the very end, as part of the last instalment, you will pay a token sum – 50p or £1 – to *purchase* the goods. Until that time they *do not* belong to you; they belong to the finance company – so you have no claim against the garage or trader because you had no contract with *him*. But you do have a claim against the finance company because the law *implies* into all hire-purchase agreements similar terms relating to the quality and fitness of goods let under such arrangements. So, your recourse is to write to the finance company pointing out the defects and asking what they are going to do about *their* property. Keep a copy of this letter. If the finance company is unhelpful and the defects were present when you bought the goods (and are not due to misuse or damage caused by wear and tear) you could consider having them repaired at your own expense. You may then be entitled to deduct the payment from your instalments – making quite sure, of course, that you write to the finance company explaining exactly what you are doing and why. Keep a copy of the letter – and always quote the reference number on the h.p. agreement in all correspondence.

182 Are you sure that I have this right? When I informed the finance company about goods going wrong, they said that as the goods were over a year old they were not responsible since the guarantee had expired.

A. A guarantee is irrelevant, at least as far as your claim for damages for breach of contract is concerned. It *may* be a measure of the sort of time you can expect goods to work as well as when they were brand new; and you do have the burden of proving (see evidence question 401/2) that what you are complaining about is due to an inherent defect. Certainly you would not be entitled to claim the price that you paid for the goods or your money back in full; but if what has gone wrong can be shown – by expert evidence, if necessary – to be unreasonable, having regard to the age of the goods, you do have a claim for some compensation. The older the goods, the harder it is to show that what went wrong was inevitable.

183 When I did what you suggested and obtained a copy of the credit reference agency file on me, I was shocked to see that there was an entry containing details of a judgment against me nearly twenty years ago. I had long since paid this off and had forgotten about it. Do you think it is reasonable for this to be on my record?

A. Credit reference agencies receive and store information about you and your credit worthiness. It is a *fact* that many years ago you had an unsatisfied judgment against you; this means that you had been sued, lost, and had not paid. You can't challenge that. So a potential lender is entitled to know that; after all, would you lend money to someone who didn't pay judgment debts? You can reasonably ask the agency to put a note on the file showing that you paid the debt off completely and have never had any other sort of judgment. But you cannot alter history.

184 Sometimes a judgment may get on the register by mistake, or because of someone letting a claim go through when he didn't think it related to him, or just ignoring it. What can one do then?

A. The first rule of litigation is: never ignore any court papers. Many people think that if they shove them in the bin or pretend that the case isn't happening, it will all solve itself. It won't. Indeed, it will help the other side to get judgment more quickly and less expensively. And the next thing you will know is the bailiff knocking on the door. If you want to contest a claim against you, then do so – in the proper way and in the limited time available to you. Get legal advice or guidance, and above all tell the court that you are defending the case. If by some slip a judgment is registered, you can tell the credit reference agency about the mistake and ask for the entry to be deleted. Again, if they won't agree you can turn to the Office of Fair Trading for help.

185 Recently I bought some goods, but when I got them home I was not happy with them. So I stopped the cheque and took them back to the shop, explaining that I thought they were defective. The shop did not agree, and when they realized the cheque had been stopped they became extremely hostile. Do I have a right to cancel or stop a cheque?

A. It all depends. It is not something which I would advocate unless you are certain about what you are doing. A trader can sue you *on the cheque* – that is, because the method of payment which you adopted has not been complied with. And he doesn't have to make any reference to the goods for which the cheque was issued. So by stopping a cheque you may be making his task much easier. Only if the defect is self-evident would you be justified in taking this course; if there is likely to be an argument about what went wrong and whose fault it was, stopping the cheque could be an expensive thing to have done. And remember that if you issued the cheque knowing that you had no funds or knowing that you were going to avoid payment for goods by stopping the cheque – you could be committing a criminal offence. So, think very hard before taking such a drastic step.

186 That is all very well; I understand about the risks involved, but I have a similar sort of situation which is causing problems. I bought goods and paid part of the price; since using them I have had lots of problems with them, and have tried to get the shop to put things right. They now say that there is no more that can be done and I must pay the balance. I am not satisfied with that and think they are just evading their responsibility. Now they have started writing threatening letters to me and have even got their solicitor chasing me. What can I do?

A. If you believe that the goods *are* defective and that you have therefore suffered a breach of contract – stand firm. Let them sue you and counterclaim for *damages*. A lot depends on the cost of the goods, the amount you paid, and the balance outstanding. After all, if you are withholding 50% when an adequate measure of compensation might be 10%, then the shop has good grounds for treating you as unreasonable. They are entitled, too, to write and ask for the money – but they must not use threats or harass you (see question 408). A solicitor's letter asking for payment is not a threat – providing it is written in normal civilized language.

187 I recently saw a car in a used-car dealer's; I asked if I could have it inspected by an independent examiner. The garage agreed, rather reluctantly, and asked me for a deposit of £10. The expert took one look at the car and told me not to waste my money. The salesman won't give me the £10 back. What can I do?

A. If the arrangement was that you wouldn't buy the car unless your man gave it the O.K., and the salesman knew this and took the deposit – if you don't go through with the deal, your money is due back. What can you do? Sue, I suppose (see question 397). If the garage belongs to one of the motor trade associations, you could try getting them to help – but shoddy, shady traders usually don't belong to anything respectable.

188 When I took my car in for a service they told me to leave it in a side street. I locked it and made the car immobile, leaving the rotor arm and the keys with reception. When I went back the next day they said the car had been stolen. I remonstrated with them and said that it was their job to safeguard my car while it was under their protection. We have got nowhere, and as I am not insured for theft I am desperate.

A. I bet you are. The law is in an odd state about this sort of obligation. When one leaves property with someone else, it is called a *bailment*. The *bailee* (the person who is given temporary possession) has an obligation to take such reasonable care of the goods as a careful man would of his own property. So if a reasonably sensible person – like yourself – leaves a vehicle in a public place in a condition in which it is difficult to drive to wait for work to be done to it, the garage is not under any greater obligation. Much turns, of course, on what was done with the car. If the rotor arm was replaced by the garage, and then the car was left in the road, you may have a claim because they had not made the car immobile. Can the garage produce the keys and the rotor arm? If yes, they are probably off the hook; if no, you have a claim.

189 Could the garage put up a notice disclaiming responsibility?

A. Yes, they could – but whether or not it had any effect would depend on its wording and its reasonableness.

190 What do you mean?

A. The wording first: for any notice to be effective it must clearly specify the limitation it is seeking to impose. If it is ambiguous the court will interpret it in the way which is least favourable to the person who is trying to rely on it. So, a sign saying 'cars parked at owner's risk' in a car-park might well not help the car-park people at all, because you could read the notice as meaning 'parked at the risk of the owner *of the car-park*', couldn't you? Or 'the management accept no responsibility for hats and coats' – could mean that they don't take responsibility for your appalling taste in choosing a purple coat! So it is vital for any trader who still thinks there is some point in putting up a notice to ensure that it does do what he wants it to. Secondly, the notice must be incorporated in the contract by being drawn to your attention before you made it or by being clearly visible to you when you made the contract. Having a sign you can only see some time later, after the money has been paid, or the job booked, or by having it in the small print on an order form you only see after the work has been completed (as so many garages do) means that it has no legal effect at all – and the trader can't rely on it.

191 Where does reasonableness come in?

A. There are a number of situations now where small print may still be legally valid if the wording is reasonable. Any term or notice by which a trader tries to avoid or limit his liability for his negligence, or by which he tries to be entitled to perform a contract in a different way or not at all – is to be tested for reasonableness before the court will allow the trader to shelter behind it. This still means that you have to sue, of course, but the onus is on the trader to try and prove that the wording *is* reasonable.

192 Does this protection extend to all negligence?

A. Where a contract term or a notice tries to avoid liability for death or injury, it will have no effect at all; the test of reasonableness is not required. If you were injured and can show that the trader – say, a holiday camp operator, or travel company, a car-park firm or a stately-home owner – *was* negligent (and this burden still rests squarely on you), he

93

would not be able to rely on this sort of notice but would have to pay you whatever compensation the court ordered.

193 Does this apply to nationalized industries?

A. Yes – with three exceptions. The Post Office is not liable to you if it is negligent in the way it deals with the post and telecommunications. This is a statutory exemption. The supply of electricity and gas are not dealt with by the law of contract, and so this part of the law does not apply. And the law does not apply to some international contracts. Apart from that, it is fairly comprehensive – so far as it goes.

194 What other limitations are there?

A. The new law only regulates the matters which are set out in the Unfair Contract Terms Act; many contract terms are not affected at all, such as those dealing with price changes, the time in which a contract is to be performed, delivery or what happens when the contract is broken by the consumer. And it only applies to contracting out of *business liability* – and so would not cover private liability, or the activities of a member's club, or even, probably, a university! And it does not extend to insurance policies or contracts for the sale of land, among others.

195 Why are gas and electricity not covered by contract?

A. Because they are statutory services. Providing you come within the rules anyone can ask to be connected to the gas or electricity main. The Gas Corporation or the Electricity Area Board is then under a statutory obligation to ensure that the energy is supplied to you. If they cut you off for no good reason, you can take them to the magistrates court and, if convicted, they will be fined. But you can't sue for breach of contract and recover damages – though the criminal law does allow compensation orders to be made in a proper case. All other things which the gas and electricity authorities do are covered by the ordinary law of contract, of course.

196 What about the railways?

A. Yes, the normal law of contract applies to railways and to the bus and airline operators. All of them have extensive rules about what their terms of business are, and often seek to exclude or limit their liability. Insofar as the offending term comes within the Unfair Contract Terms Act, the test of reasonableness will apply. And they must take adequate steps to ensure that the existence of the contract terms (and bye-laws) are drawn to your attention before the contract is made.

197 As a small trader I keep receiving documents through the post which look like invoices. They often come from abroad but relate to directories, which, so the document says, are to be published in this country. I don't have to pay, do I?

A. No. This form of *inertia selling* was rife in the early Seventies and was a cause of considerable loss to firms. The law was changed to make it illegal, but it did not go far enough, and in 1975 a further change was made. Any document must now be on white paper and must carry notices in red print stating 'This is not a demand for payment, there is no obligation to pay' and 'this is not a bill'. So, if you receive a document which is an unsolicited invoice throw it away if it contains these red notices; if it does not, you could tell your Trading Standards department which has the responsibility for enforcing the law.

198 Is sending goods by post to a person 'inertia selling' if he has not asked for them?

A. Yes it is; and it is regulated by the law, too. Sending what are called *unsolicited goods* is not a crime (unless they relate to sexual techniques), but the recipient has some rights. You can either write to the firm that sent the goods asking them to come and collect them within one month; or you can sit tight and wait for six months. At the end of either period the goods become yours to do with as you want. You have been given legal title to the goods which would otherwise not be yours. You should note that this does not apply to goods which are sent to you as part of a business you are carrying on.

199 I run a shoe repair shop and people are often bringing things in for repair, leaving them, and never coming back! I have a cupboard in the back of the shop which is stuffed full of old shoes. Apart from the inconvenience, it is expensive, of course, because the shoes and handbags have been repaired, but I haven't been paid. What can I do?

A. There are two things you can do – the first of which is obviously better from all points of view. Make it a term of your business that goods which have been repaired, but not collected, within a reasonable period – say, a month – will be disposed of. This way you can lawfully deal with other people's property and pass a good title to anyone who buys the goods. It is important to ensure that the notice containing this wording, or the document containing it, is clearly drawn to the customers' attention before the contract is made. You could put it in the document which you hand to the customer, providing it is plain that this *is* a contract document and not just a simple receipt. Get legal advice on the form of words and the method of letting the customer know. The other way is to deal with the thing from the opposite end. A new law enables a trader who is stuck with other people's property to demand collection and payment or to sell it, providing he complies with the rules laid down. This needs notices to be sent, and at least three months to have elapsed. The Schedule to the Torts (Interference with Goods) Act

1977 sets out the procedure. It is a useful new measure of trader protection, although it means that records must be kept of the customer's name and address. If you don't, you may have to apply to the court for an order for sale – which is a waste of time and a needless expense.

200 What happens to the money I get for selling the goods which are uncollected?

A. It belongs to the true owner, of course, but you are entitled to pay your own bill out of the proceeds and then keep the balance against the day the chap comes in and asks for his brogues.

201 Do I have to pay for the sweets that my children take off the counter at a supermarket checkout?

A. How old are children? If they are tiny you may have to, because it could be said that they were directly under your control. But as they get older, it becomes increasingly difficult to say that it is your responsibility. You may have a moral obligation – but the law isn't concerned with morals. It is sometimes overlooked that children are people and have rights and obligations. The shop could try and sue the child for non-payment; would a court say that a supermarket which put sweets carefully within sight and reach of a child had brought the situation upon itself? I don't know.

202 Does the same apply to breakages in shops by a child?

A. Yes. It is the responsibility of the person who did it. If you told your toddler to 'go and smash the glasses, dear', the trader would have a claim against you! But if it is an action by the child himself, even though you were holding his other hand, the loss would fall on the trader. Proving negligence against a child is not easy; a child is treated as an individual, and is presumed to have a lesser degree of know-ledge of the consequences of his actions than a teenager or an adult.

203 What if the breakage is by me, rather than my child?

A. The shop has to prove that you were negligent; so, if you pick up a bottle and it drops through your fingers because they are cold – then there is no fault on your part, and no liability. If you drop it deliberately, there is. If the breakage occurs because the stopper is loose or the container is sticky – *you* may well have a claim against the shop if your other goods are damaged or your clothing stained. The only way a shop can try to prevent this loss from falling on itself is to display conspicuously a notice telling you not to touch things. If you disobey this notice, the trader can take action against you.

204 Last year I left a ring for repair and cleaning at a jeweller's. He gave me a ticket for it which had no small print on it – just his name and a number. When I went back to collect it, I was told there had been a burglary and the ring had gone, along with most of the other things he had in the place. I sympathized with him, but asked for the value of the ring. He told me it was nothing to do with him, and his insurance company have refused to pay, too. I just don't understand this.

A. Nor do many people. Unfortunately the jeweller is probably correct. His is a *bailee* of your ring (see question 188) and has to take reasonable care of it while it is in his custody. So he should have proper thief-proof locks, bars and shutters, a safe for valuable items, and possibly a burglar alarm and even a link with the police station – depending on the value of his stock. If he takes most of these precautions, then he will have done all that he has to; then, unless you can show that he was negligent – like leaving the door open, or the key in the lock – you will have no claim against him if there was a burglary. The same thing applies to fire or other loss; negligence by the bailee has to be proved for the victim to have a claim for the cost of goods damaged or lost. It means, of course, that *you* should be insured – and check that the policy extends to your property when it is *not* in your house.

205 How does one establish the amount of compensation to be paid for goods which are damaged or destroyed – say at the cleaners?

A. You must understand that the only thing you can claim is the value of the goods at the time they were lost or damaged, *not* the replacement value or what they originally cost you. This is often bad news because your favourite table-cloth may have been a family treasure but as a tablecloth it was x years old and so worth only a few pence – not the £50 you would have to pay to replace it. Cleaners and launderers who belong to a trade association have a compensation-scheme – providing you can establish fault on their part.

206 I understand that there can be a claim against a credit-card company if things go wrong. Is this right, and how does it work?

A. There are only two credit-card companies in this country – Access and Barclaycard. Apart from the cards issued by companies for use in their shops, other things which may have the appearance of credit cards are not, because they do not allow you to defer payment of the outstanding bill and be charged interest. So, the present remedy which exists is limited to Access and Barclaycard. Where there is a breach of contract by the seller of goods or person who provides you with services for which you paid by a credit card, then you can take up your complaint with the trader *or* the bank. Your contract must have been for a cash price between £30 and £10,000 – so small purchases are outside the scope of the provision. And just what you can recover depends on whether your credit card was issued before or after 1 July 1977. If before, the banks will only compensate you up to the price on the credit card voucher; if after, the potential liability is unlimited. This means that there are two categories of cardholder; not something about which the Office of Fair Trading is enthusiastic.

207 In a large store the other day I was stopped and accused of stealing; a large woman insisted that I went to the manager's office, and I had my bag taken from me and emptied out. I was kept for some time before another person came in and told me I could go, without even apologizing. I was most upset.

A. I am not surprised; and I hope that you will take legal advice. Anyone who has reason to believe that a criminal offence has been committed can make enquiries. The danger is if you are wrong; the person accused can take action in the civil court for damages for *false imprisonment* and *trespass*. Preventing you from leaving a shop is almost certainly false imprisonment because you are not free to go about your business. And looking in your handbag or shopping basket without your genuine consent will be trespass. If you are put in fear of physical violence, that is assault. So, the shop which treated you in such a cavalier way is asking to be sued for damages for all these things. Take legal advice, as I have suggested, and consider applying for *legal aid* (see question 416). The shop would do well to get advice too.

208 You have avoided dealing with *guarantees*. Why? And just what are they?

A. I am not happy about guarantees, not because they do not sometimes offer useful help, but because they confuse people. Go back to question 145 and question 173, and you will see what I mean. Your contract is with the retailer, and it is to him that you should turn if things go wrong; but many people don't; they believe that the guarantee gives them legal rights against the manufacturer; the retailer will tell them to use the guarantee; no one really knows where they stand. A guarantee is a bit of cardboard with writing on. It may offer you the chance of having things put right within a limited time – a year usually – often on terms that you pay carriage or labour or parts, or some, or all; and possibly under conditions such as, that you have bought from an approved agent; that the goods were bought for the full list price, and not at a discount; that they are returned in the container. These restrictions are most unreasonable and deflect the burden of putting goods in the right state from the trader who sold them. They also impose an arbitrary period of a year as the expected life of goods which fails to take use into account. Unfairness is caused by defects occurring in the fifty-third week; some firms cheat by not taking up problems which happen in the fifty-first week because they were not notified until the year had expired. Finally – you don't see the things until you get the goods home and dig about in the packaging. They have no legal status because there is no consideration – no value passing between the buyer and the company issuing the guarantee. So, there is nothing to enforce or sue about. As to the value of the guarantee – it depends entirely on what it offers. I have indicated some of the shortcomings; there can be benefits which make it worth while filling in the card and posting it off. It is really up to you – and much depends on the type of goods, anyway. Sorry not to be more forthcoming.

209 When there is a breach of contract and goods are defective, what can I claim for compensation?

A. If the goods are defective virtually on purchase, you can reject them and claim back your money, plus any other out-of-pocket expense you have incurred. But if you have *accepted* the goods (see question 172) you will NOT be able to get your money back in full – but only the cost of repair or adjustment. This is the limit of your *damages* – plus out-of-pocket expenses – like fares, petrol, the loss of a day's pay. And if the goods are a write-off and you can only re-purchase them at a higher price, the difference between the prices is also an item you can claim as part of your damages.

5

EMPLOYMENT

**210 I was offered a job after an interview and went along on
the agreed day to start work. To my amazement, the man who
had interviewed me said that he had changed his mind, and
there wasn't a job after all. What is my position?**

A. There is a breach of contract by the firm. A contract of
employment is made in the same way as any other – by an
offer of work being accepted by the applicant in writing or
by word of mouth. Once that has happened, then there is a
legal relationship between you, and a breach – by either
side – gives rise to a claim for *damages* – compensation. The
trouble is that your damages may be very small because any
employer can dismiss a person without any notice in the
first four weeks (unless the contract made between you
provides differently). You can be shown the door and your
only comeback is a claim for a week's pay. And if you had
incurred any expenses specifically in connection with the
employment – like moving house or travelling costs – these
could be claimed, too.

**211 Would it be different if the job for which I had been em-
ployed had been for a fixed period of, say, three months or
two years?**

A. Yes, because then the period of work would have been
certain and – unless the contract provided for notice (and
this sort of contract often does not) – could not have been
ended prematurely. In such a case, you would have a claim

103

for three months' or two years' pay. That is why you hear about huge *golden handshakes* being given to senior managers when they get the boot. Not because they are splendid chaps to be rewarded, but because they were prudent enough to ensure that the contract (or service agreement as it may be called) was for a definite period without notice.

212 Do I have to be given a written contract?

A. No, you do not (unless you are an apprentice). A contract of employment can be made by word of mouth, and often is. There may be a letter setting out the offer of work and the terms and conditions, and occasionally there is a written contract. But because so many jobs are offered verbally, there is no record of what the terms are, and so Parliament has tried to protect workers. A worker MUST be given a written statement of the main terms and conditions of the employment within thirteen weeks of starting work. (The only exception to this is where there is a written contract containing the information required by law.) This written statement is NOT a contract of employment. That will have been made before you start work. But it does provide very good evidence of what the contract was all about.

213 What sort of information must the 'written statement of the terms and conditions' contain?

A. · The names of the employer and worker;
   · The date the employment started;
   · Whether employment with a previous employer counts as continuous;
   · The scale or rate of pay; or the method of calculating pay;
   · The intervals at which payment is made (weekly, monthly, etc.);
   · Any terms relating to hours of work;

104

- Any terms about holidays, sickness (including sick pay) pensions and pension schemes;
- The length of notice on both sides; and the date of expiry if the contract is for a fixed term;
- Job description or title;
- Disciplinary rules; or reference to a document (like a rule book) in which this will be found;
- Name or description of the person to turn to if aggrieved by disciplinary action;
- What other steps can be taken on disciplinary matters.

214 Does all this have to go in?

A. All the categories have to be completed by the employer; but if no provision is made in a particular section (if, for example, there are no holidays, or holiday pay), that fact must be put in the written statement. And reference to a rule-book or other document – which *must* be available – is adequate to draw your attention to the terms.

215 What happens if I am not given a written statement?

A. Nothing very effective, I am afraid. You can refer the matter to an industrial tribunal (see question 251) which can decide what the main terms ought to have been; but a tribunal cannot award you compensation for the employer's failure to give you the written statement. So, if you feel that you have lost pay or benefits as a result of not having the written statement, you will have to sue in the county court (see question 397).

216 What is the point of making employers give these notices if you cannot do anything if they don't?

A. A good question; it was originally a criminal offence not to give a written statement; but that was changed to this empty remedy of going to a tribunal. The point really is that employers ought to comply, and many firms which used not to give any written terms of employment now do so. Trade associations prepare forms which they suggest their members use. It is obviously good sense for both sides of the labour front to know what the worker's job is and all the other terms. It prevents battles and needless cost later. You should also insist that your employer gives you a written statement. But don't think that it is your *contract*.

217 Is there anyone to whom a written statement need not be given?

A. Yes; people who have been given a written contract of employment which includes all the matters set out in answer to question 213; people who work less than sixteen hours a week (unless they have worked for at least five years for at least eight hours a week); registered dock workers and sea-men; people who work abroad; crown servants; and if you start work again for the same employer within six months.

218 For years I have been paid weekly in cash. I am used to that way and make all my budget plans accordingly. Now my firm have said that I will be paid monthly straight into a bank account. I do not like this idea at all, but they have told me that if I do not like it, I can always leave. Can you help?

A. The way in which you are paid is a basic term of your contract. It should be included in your *written statement* to emphasize that it is important. Your employer cannot alter the contract without your agreement. If he does so, then he breaks the contract, and you are entitled to compensation. You could treat the contract as ended and claim unfair dismissal (see question 242); or you could soldier on and go to court for an order that the firm goes on paying you in the agreed way. Or you could let them sack you and again claim unfair dismissal. The first thing to do, of course, is to talk to

106

someone responsible at work and try to get them to see your problem. Or get on to your union representative if you have one. Finally a solicitor's letter to the firm might make them see sense.

219 Can I insist on being paid in cash?

A. Theoretically, yes. The law says that a worker is entitled to be paid in coin of the realm. Certainly you are not allowed to be paid in kind or by tokens or anything which is not money based. Nowadays, if you ask to be paid by cheque or by a direct credit to a bank account, this is in order; and if you are told at the outset and accept it, you cannot complain. But an employer cannot insist on changing the method of payment against your wishes.

220 What is the relevance of 'continuity of employment' in the list of things to be set out in the written statement?

A. A number of rights and benefits are available to a worker whose period of employment has been *continuous* for a set period of time. In other words, *time* is a qualifying factor. For example, you must have been continuously employed: for twenty-six weeks, to be able to make a complaint of unfair dismissal (see question 242) to an industrial tribunal (see question 251); for two years, to qualify for maternity pay or redundancy pay; for five years, if you are a part-timer, to get certain basic rights. While there is a presumption of continuity, it can be broken. And if that happens, you have to start all over again. A change of employment usually means that continuity is broken. But it is not if the firm is taken over by someone else; or if nationalization (or state acquisition) takes place; or an employer dies (or a partner retires), but the firm still goes on trading; or if you switch jobs to an associated company. But if the firm goes into liquidation, or your employer is made bankrupt, continuity is broken, even though you have certain rights (see question 259). Other things stop time running without breaking the continuity. Sickness for up to twenty-six weeks, a strike, pregnancy and maternity leave, for example. So if you are off for twelve weeks, your employment is continuous, but twelve weeks have to be added on to any qualifying period.

221 My contract of employment says that the employer can deduct fines if I am late, or break the firm's rules, or damage the goods being made. This has been the case for many years, but most of us believe that it is out of date and not enforceable. Is this so?

A. No, it is NOT. The rules about deductions and fines are very tight, and the law says that they must be spelt out in the contract of employment to be effective. But so long as they *are* correctly stated, then the firm can fine you. So fines are leviable for damage to goods or stock, interruption to his business or even for disobeying a rule to 'observe good order and decorum' – in that case, dancing on a factory floor during the dinner break! You must be given written details of the misdemeanour for which you are being fined – and the deduction must be fair and reasonable. And this applies to shop assistants (which includes delivery roundsmen) as well as to factory workers. So watch out!

222 I am a manager for a shop owned by a chain. My hours are long, and I think anti-social – so does my wife. A flat goes with the job for which rent is deducted from my pay. If I leave, can the firm demand the flat back?

A. Yes. You are not a Rent Act protected tenant because the accommodation goes with the job. If you don't leave it the firm can sue you for possession and also *damages* for *trespass*, because you have no right to be there. They cannot just sling you and your family into the street, though, without a court order to evict you. The same lack of security applies if you didn't pay rent, or if you had been offered a 'job for life with rent-free accommodation' and the job was ended.

223 I have been asked to do some private work in my own time. It will be exactly the same sort of thing I do at work, and I shall be paid. I have heard it said that I should tell my boss or clear it with him. My contract says nothing about it. What should I do?

A. It often comes as a shock to people to be told that they cannot work in any substantial way for someone else, even in their spare time, if what they are doing clashes with their duty to their employer. So you have to look at the job you have been asked to do. Does it clash with anything your ordinary job entails? Is the person a customer of your boss? How much will you be paid? Does your boss know about it? Do other people do private work? If it is a one-off or occasional activity, then probably there is no problem; but if you are working for an existing customer – competing, in effect, with your own employer – then you may be in difficulty. In theory, the money you receive could be claimed by your firm. The sensible thing is to talk it over with your boss, for most people are quite happy that their staff do what they like in their spare time. Sometimes the contract makes specific mention of this; you may be able to earn so much and keep it, but above a limit account to the employer.

224 Following on from the last question, if I decide to quit my job, can I take customers with me?

A. You can compete with your former firm once you have left unless there is a clause in your contract stopping you from competing. This type of clause may well be void (of no legal effect) unless the employer can show that it is reasonable; if it is, he can stop you trying to persuade former customers to change to you, or stop you opening up within a short distance from his place of business. Also, you cannot canvass customers before you leave or copy out lists of customers from the firm's records. Once you have gone, however, you are entitled to canvass and to make up lists from memory; you cannot simply photostat everything and take it with you, however great the temptation is! But do look out for a non-competing clause. If there is one, get legal advice on it.

225 During my work for a repair firm I made an invention which is of considerable value. How do I go about exploiting this?

A. Until very recently you would have had no claim to the invention at all, whether it was made in your spare time or not. It belonged to your employer, and he could – and often did – take the benefit of it without much, if anything, in the way of a reward for your ingenuity. Things have now radically altered. Where the invention is made at work, or closely connected with your work, it is to be treated as belonging to your employer. There is now a scheme of compensation for workers which will enable you to ask the Comptroller-General of Patents to rule on the invention and to apportion the benefit of the invention between you and your employer, the intention being that you should get a fair share of the benefit. In other cases the invention is deemed to you – so you get the credit.

226 My company has taken to searching staff and their cars on the pretext of 'security'. And there is now a notice in the car park stating that all cars are liable to random searches ◄ without notice. Can I refuse to take part?

A. It depends entirely on your contract of employment and the rules which the firm have – providing that they are incorporated into your contract. If these say that searches take place, then it is lawful and you refuse at your peril. But should there be *no* contract term, any search of an employee or a vehicle is a trespass which would give rise to a claim for damages. Of course, there is an exception where the firm have reason to believe that a crime may have been committed; even then, should they be wrong, an action may lie for *trespass*. If you *agree* to a search, you have no redress.

110

227 Is it reasonable, in these days of equality, for an employer to insist on female workers wearing skirts or dresses and banning trousers?

A. Again, it depends on the contract or the firm's rules, and on the type of business. It might be very unreasonable to expect a girl working in all weathers on a garage forecourt to wear a dress; equally, it might be unsuitable for a saleslady to wear dungarees in the perfumery department of a posh shop. Equality hasn't really got anything to do with the right of an employer to insist on a reasonably clean and smart staff. In many jobs protective clothing has to be provided.

228 What rights do women have when they are pregnant or wanting to take time off to have a baby?

A. For a start, their entitlements are unique to their sex. Men have nothing similar! The woman has two rights. First to job security – not to be dismissed simply because she is pregnant (so long as she has worked for twenty-six weeks), coupled with the right to return to the job after the baby is born. To qualify for this right, she must be at work up to the eleventh week before the baby is due and have been *continuously employed* for two years. She must tell the employer (in writing if he requires) *at least* three weeks before she leaves that she intends to stop work, at the same time stating that she intends to return to work after the baby is born. It is vital to get this notification right, and to do it at the correct time. Being out of time – even by a day – loses the right to return to work. So don't vacillate. The second benefit is the right to maternity pay. The qualifying conditions are as before, except that notice of less than three weeks may be given in *special circumstances*. Maternity pay sounds great, but it only amounts to 9/10 of normal weekly pay for the first six weeks the woman is away, less the state maternity allowance whether she actually gets this or not. Some firms, in fact, pay more than this under the contract of employment – and obviously have to meet that obligation rather than pay the lower amount.

229 How does a woman exercise her right to return?

A. The date of her return is up to her, providing it is not more than twenty-nine weeks after the baby's birth. At least one week's notice of her intention to return must be given to the employer. He may put the return off for up to four weeks if reasons are given (like someone else being employed as a temp. to do her work).

230 What happens if a woman is dismissed because she is pregnant?

A. That will be treated as an unfair dismissal and enable her to complain to an industrial tribunal (see question 251). Only if the employer can show that he offered suitable alternative work which the girl refused can he avoid being liable to pay compensation or reinstate her.

231 What if she gives notice of her intention to return but doesn't come back?

A. If the decision is hers, then she has no claim for anything. But if the boss refuses to let her return, or the job she did no longer exists, she will be able to claim unfair dismissal or redundancy.

232 Does the temp. employed to fill her place have job security?

A. Not if she was told at the outset that the job *was* an in-fill for a woman who was temporarily absent having a baby. Giving her notice would not be unfair dismissal.

233 How do I qualify for state maternity allowance?

A. You must be a woman, you must be pregnant, and you must usually have paid full-rate national insurance contributions *yourself* during the preceding tax year. There are very complicated rules about this, and you ought to safeguard your own position by getting leaflet NI17A from the Social Security Office. There is a flat-rate allowance to which earnings-related additions can be made in a proper case.

234 Do men get paternity leave?

A. Not at present, though there has been discussion about introducing this, at least for a limited period.

235 You have mentioned redundancy. What is it, and how does one qualify for redundancy pay?

A. Redundancy is losing your job: when an employer stops business; or ceases carrying on work at the place you usually work; or when the type of job is no longer available either generally or at a particular place. Redundancy pay is a lump sum which is paid by an employer to a worker who is made redundant. To qualify, the worker must be over eighteen have worked for a *continuous* period of two years, and be under sixty-five (if a man) or sixty (if a woman).

236 Can I get redundancy pay if my job is no longer available for some other reason – like my ill health or because I can't do it?

A. Not usually; you must have been dismissed, and the dismissal must be related to redundancy.

237 My husband's firm decided that it would shift its business from Kent to the North. We didn't want to move, so he found another job locally. Can he claim redundancy pay?

A. Yes; his decision to leave was because of the termination of his job in Kent. It was, therefore, caused by redundancy. He was acting reasonably in refusing their offer of alternative employment hundreds of miles away. He can apply to a tribunal (see question 251) for payment if the firm won't pay up on their own.

238 I was told that if I left work, I would not get a refund of my pension and superannuation contributions, but these would be transferred to my new job. Can the firm do this?

A. Yes, because the terms of the pension scheme allow them to do so, and these terms are incorporared in your contract of employment.

239 When I left work I should have been given a Tax Form P45 and my National Insurance details. I have still not received my P45, and the new tax office has put me on an emergency code number. Is there anything I can do?

A. The regulations say that an employer shall make a copy of the tax details and 'shall deliver it to the worker on the day the employment ceases'. But it does not say what happens if the employer fails to do this; it is not one of the criminal offences under the Taxes Acts. The simplest thing is to try and persuade your new tax office to get in touch with the former one and find out the details from it. And that may take time, I am afraid.

240 What is the minimum period of full-time employment before one can claim *unfair dismissal*?

A. Usually twenty-six weeks' *continuous employment*; it is less for some medical suspension cases, and nil for people who are dismissed for trade union activities or membership. It is five years for part-timers working eight or more hours a week (unless it is related to trade union matters when the number of hours worked are irrelevant).

241 Is there an upper age limit?

A. Yes; sixty-five for men, and sixty for women – but a recent decision has improved the woman's position by saying that it will be sixty-five where that is the normal retirement age for a woman in a particular employment.

242 What exactly is unfair dismissal?

A. Do not be deluded into believing that it has anything to do with the ordinary dictionary meaning of those words. Indeed, a judge once said that it was 'not a commonsense expression capable of being understood by the man in the street'! Four things have to be looked at. First, was there a dismissal? The worker has to prove that there was, and what its date was. Secondly, what was the reason for the dismissal? The employer has to prove the principal reason or to show the facts causing the dismissal. Thirdly, all the circumstances have to be considered. Finally, did the employer act reasonably?

243 Are some dismissals automatically unfair?

A. Yes. A worker who has *spent convictions*, who is sacked because of them; a woman who is pregnant, or absent having a baby, whose job is ended; trade union membership or activities; unfair redundancy. All these are automatically treated as unfair.

244 I had a fight with my boss and knocked him out. Not very surprisingly, I was sacked – but the reason given was bad timekeeping. That is one thing that no one can possibly complain about. My record is first class. Was I fairly dismissed?

A. Not if that was the reason which the employer wrote down and relied on. You would be able to show that you were not a bad timekeeper, and the employer would not be allowed to bring up the fight. He was foolish. The correct reason would have made his action perfectly reasonable.

245 My weekly pay packet often contains little or no information about what money is being deducted. When I ask I am told it is right and that I must accept what I am given and not complain. I don't want to make trouble, but I do want to know exactly what is being taken off.

A. Of course you do. Until recently your employer *could* do what he wanted. Now the law has been changed. Everyone who is an employee (except spouses, and part-timers working less than eight hours) is entitled to an itemized payslip. This must state: the gross amount of the pay; the amount of any *fixed deductions*; the amount of *variable deductions*; the net pay; and the amount and method of payment of wages paid in different ways.

246 What are these fixed and variable deductions and what is their relevance?

A. *Fixed* ones are those which are the same or change infrequently – like National Insurance contributions, union and club subscriptions, savings and court orders. A statement of fixed deductions can be given, and then the total shown on the payslip – because you can refer to the statement to see how they are made up. *Variable* deductions are those which vary, e.g. tax, sickness benefit, fines. Each and every one must be given at each pay date.

247 What can I do if I don't get a proper payslip?

A. You can apply to an industrial tribunal (see question 251), and if there is a decision that you were not given a payslip which met the legal rules, the tribunal can order the employer to repay to you all unnotified deductions for up to thirteen weeks immediately prior to your application.

248 Earlier you mentioned the reasons for a dismissal being given. I thought that there was no legal requirement to give the reason why someone was sacked?

A. The law was altered in 1976. You can now ask for a written statement of the reasons which must be given to you within fourteen days. You must have been *continuously employed* for twenty-six weeks, and you must have been given notice, or dismissed without notice, or a fixed term contract must have expired without renewal. If the employer doesn't comply with your request, you can apply to an industrial tribunal (see question 251) which can award you two weeks' pay.

249 Is there a legal requirement for an employer to give a reference?

A. No; there is still no obligation for a former employer to give one.

250 Unfair dismissal presumably relates to a breach of contract by the employer. Can I also claim compensation if the action of my boss leads me to pack in the job; in other words when I am victimized by my fellow workers and by foreman?

A. There was a time when I could have said ye the wide interpretation of conduct forci introduced in 1974 has been severely narr

Court. The concept of being forced out by the actions of an employer is called *constructive dismissal* (that means, what they did was so bad that you were justified in quitting). The current view of constructive dismissal is that what you are complaining of must be in itself a breach of contract by the employer. So, a cumulative series of nastinesses may not be enough to be a breach of contract. You have to be able to point to at least one specific event and say 'that broke my contract'; even if it is in itself a trivial thing, when combined with the systematic victimization, you may be home and dry. It is always worth getting legal advice on the matter.

251 What exactly is an industrial tribunal, and who sits on it?

A. It is an independent body set up by Parliament to deal with practically all the employment rights and remedies created by the legislation since 1962. There are tribunals all over the country. Each consists of three members: one, the chairman, is legally qualified; the other two represent trade unions and employers.

252 I imagine that legal aid and solicitors are available to help me bring a case?

A. You can and should get legal advice; or if you belong to a trade union, get help from that source. But *legal aid* is not available to [...] proceedings before a tribunal. This is [...] employers very often are legally [...] is an imbalance in the way a case is [...] trade union representatives who [...] very experienced and will be as [...] people who do not have the [...] cannot afford a solicitor, [...] tribunals are much less [...] sent quite an ordeal for a [...] ills or experience of public

253 Can't I get legal aid at all?

A. You can use the *Green Form* for the preparation of the case; a solicitor can see you and your witnesses and help you prepare a case. But the Green Form will not extend to his appearing and speaking for you. If you want him to do that you will have to pay him.

254 How can this unfairness be justified?

A. It cannot. And the government almost certainly recognizes it. At the moment a Royal Commission is looking at legal services generally, and may well make recommendations about extending legal aid to tribunals; remember it is not only industrial tribunals for which you cannot get legal aid. The only comfort for you is that there is usually no order made for a loser to pay the winner's costs – unless the tribunal thinks you have been very unreasonable or have made the whole thing up – or wasted time by delaying or not turning up for a hearing.

255 Do I have to be present? The whole thing seems most alarming.

A. No, you don't *have* to be present. The procedure works like this. You state your case in writing; this is sent to the other side who reply, then everything is sent to a Conciliation Officer who looks at the whole picture. If he thinks there is a chance of sorting the thing out, he will try and intercede putting the legal position to each side. Very often he can satisfy an employer that he is in the wrong – or tell a worker that he has no chance of success – and so resolve the case. But if he can't, then the case goes before a tribunal after each side has seen the other's case in writing and all relevant documents have also been produced and inspected.

256 Is there any time limit for bringing a case?

A. YES, there is. Three months from the dismissal date is the golden rule, from which there are practically no exceptions at all. Even if you get wrong advice or just overlook the date, that is tough. So, the moral is to get on with the preparation and legal side of your case immediately. Delay can be fatal.

257 What sort of thing can an industrial tribunal do if I win a case of unfair dismissal?

A. It can award you compensation or direct that you be given back your old job or a similar one.

258 Are there any drawbacks?

A. Yes. Your conduct will be taken into account and may substantially reduce the compensation. So, even though you may score a points victory, the tribunal may think that you brought a lot of the trouble on yourself and can penalize you by reducing the money it awards.

259 What is the position of a worker if the company he works for goes into liquidation? Or if an individual employer is made bankrupt?

A. In each case the immediate legal consequence is the same. The contract of employment is ended forthwith. You have rights to claim unpaid wages and accrued holiday pay either as a creditor of the employer or by using the rights given you by the employment laws. These enable you to claim up to eight weeks' wages and up to six weeks' holiday pay, plus any outstanding award from a tribunal. If the insolvent employer does not have the funds available, or if

120

no payment is made to you within six months, you can ask the Department of Employment to make a payment to you.

260 I am a driver for my firm and I was recently involved in a crash. Although I don't think I was to blame, the other driver has started a court case against me and the company. Why should I be named, as it wasn't my lorry but the firm's?

A. Because you were the driver who – they say – caused the accident. It is therefore you who are primarily responsible; but your employers are *vicariously liable*; that is, they accept that because you were driving about their business they will carry the can. Strictly, if you were fully to blame, they would have a claim against *you* to indemnify them for the damages they have to pay out. It is also important to note that if you were using the lorry for your own purpose – say at the week-end – or if you were not a driver but were merely helping out someone who was a driver, then you would be liable in full yourself.

261 I am an agent for a company and go round selling on the doorstep. The company goes to great lengths to emphasize that I am not an employee, and they pay me a commission on sales but not a salary. What is my position in reality?

A. You are not an employee. You are an independent contractor providing services to the company for which they pay you commission based on your sales. So you have no job security, no right to go to a tribunal if you fall out, and no right to redundancy or other benefits. On the other hand, you will have a contract with the company which you can invoke if they treat you badly, subject to the terms in it about notice on either side.

262 Can I be sacked on the spot, without any warning or notice?

121

A. Only if what you have done is something very serious indeed, like stealing from your employer, or breaking clear orders relating to your work, or if you are completely incompetent. What is complained of must go to the root of your contract and be related to your work. It would be unreasonable to sack you if you were charged with – but as yet not convicted of – a crime. And even if you were convicted, that would not be a reason to dismiss you summarily unless the crime was relevant to your employment.

263 Is there anything that can be done if I, as an employer, want to sack someone?

A. To defeat a complaint of unfair dismissal, you must be able to show that you acted *reasonably*. A dismissal on the spot for something which is not very serious would be asking for trouble. But if you follow a step by step procedure for dealing with workpeople who don't follow the rules, you may well be acting reasonably. An employer should have a disciplinary code which is available to all staff to see so that everyone knows where they stand. If you don't, then you should adopt the Code of Practice recommended by the Advisory Conciliation and Arbitration Service (ACAS) and available from H.M.S.O.

264 What does this say, and what is its legal force, if any?

A. It has no legal force, as such; but it is a document to which regard is had by tribunals, and if you *do not* follow it (or something very like it) you will be treated as unreasonable. It provides a procedure by stages: minor offences – a formal oral warning; a written warning if the thing is serious; notice of the consequences of further offences; if there is further trouble – a final written warning, informing that dismissal may follow (or some other penalty, like a transfer); final step – transfer, suspension without pay (if the contract allows for this). An appeal mechanism must be included and the matter dealt with by someone other than the offender's immediate superior. And you should follow elementary rules of justice – like letting the person have his say and be represented by a union or work colleague.

265 I am a woman worker doing the same work alongside men, but I do not get the same pay. Isn't this discrimination?

A. Probably. The law says that women must get the same pay and conditions as men for the *same or broadly similar* work. Of course, you must be roughly equivalent in terms of age, experience and qualifications (if any).

266 How does the law deal with sex discrimination?

A. In theory, it stops it; at least where six or more workers are employed. You can still discriminate in smaller places. What is hoped is that a large measure of commonsense will be applied in both the selection of staff and the terms and conditions which are imposed on them. If you believe that you didn't get a job because of your sex, or that your terms of employment are different from those of male colleagues, you can apply to an industrial tribunal for a ruling. And you can inform the Equal Opportunities Commission.

267 What happens if you are dissatisfied with a decision of an industrial tribunal?

A. You can appeal on a point of law only to the Employment Appeal Tribunal – which is a branch of the High Court with a presiding judge and two assessors. The case is reviewed, the Appeal Tribunal looking at the judgment and the evidence, as well as hearing submissions from both sides. You must give notice of appeal within forty-two days of the decision of the industrial tribunal.

268 Is there any minimum period of notice to be given to end a contract of employment?

A. There is; and it depends whether you are a boss or worker. After four weeks' employment, an employer has to give at least one weeks' notice; after two years' employment, the minimum notice is one week for each year of work (e.g. six weeks after six years) up to a maximum of twelve weeks after twelve years. A worker has to give one week's notice after he has worked for four weeks, but this never increases. If the contract of employment lays down longer periods of notice on the employer's side, these have to be followed. But, apparently, it doesn't matter that the worker is supposed to give longer notice than a week; that is all he need give and all the employer can insist on.

269 My twelve-year-old son wants to take on a paper round, but I am not sure that he can be employed so young. What are the rules?

A. No child can be employed: so long as he is under thirteen; before school closing time; before 7 a.m. or after 7 p.m. for more than two hours on a schoolday or a Sunday; that is the basic law. But regulations may be made, or bye-laws by the local council, allowing parents to employ children, and also permitting not more than one hour's work before school. So, it is very probable that your local council may have made a bye-law allowing paperboys/girls to do their dawn patrol. But check first. The thirteen age limit is absolute. Below that age employment is illegal (unless the child is employed by the parent).

270 What rights do children who are properly employed have?

A. Virtually none. They are not entitled to any of the provisions about notice, job security or pay. They can be hired and fired at will. It seems odd to me that a society that is so keen on protecting practically everyone in sight should ignore children; or, even worse, make laws and then drive a steam-roller through them.

271 Am I entitled to holiday pay from my firm?

A. Not unless your contract says so. In some types of work Orders have been made laying down minimum wages and holiday pay schemes. And some trade union agreements deal with it too. But apart from these you have no *right* to holiday pay. There is just one exception; a factory occupier must allow Bank Holidays, Good Friday and Christmas Day to every woman and young person employed there. And he can alter that by notice. The European Social Charter says that all workers should have public holidays and two weeks' annual holiday with pay. Roll on the day!

272 I work at home making things for a firm. I get paid according to the number of articles I assemble. I don't think I get a very good deal; sometimes the rate is only a few pence per hour. Is there anything I can do?

A. Home-workers are sometimes ripped off by employers. You could ask the Low Pay Unit if you come within any scheme of wages; you may well come within a Wages Council Order in which case it is worth asking the Wages Inspectorate to investigate whether you are being underpaid. Recent surveys have shown that many people do not receive what they should.

273 What do the Wages Inspectors do?

A. They enforce the Orders which have been made for specific types of employment where minimum wage levels (and holiday pay, etc.) are laid down. If they find that an employer is underpaying his workers he can be taken to court; and, far more to the point, he can be ordered to repay arrears. Your local Employment Office should be able to tell you the phone-number of the Wages Inspector; or look in the phone book under 'W'.

6

WILLS

274 How do I make a will, and why should I bother anyway?

A. It is tidy and sensible to make a will. It saves trouble and confusion after your death and prevents family disputes. If you want to set up complicated trusts for your surviving spouse and children, then go to a solicitor and get the job done properly. On the other hand, if you want to make sure that your spouse, or your children, or the cats' home get what you have, you can make a will. Will forms are available from stationers, or you can just write it out on a clean sheet of paper. There are books available (see page 209) which contain advice and guidance.

275 What should I put in it?

A. It is important to ensure that an executor is named (and make sure he wants to act), that there are no crossings out, that the will is dated and signed by you, and that the signature is witnessed by TWO people present at the same time. Neither a witness nor his spouse can benefit under a will, so make certain that whoever does witness your signature is not likely to have any claim. A person who makes a will is called a *testator*.

276 What happens if I die without making one?

A. You die *intestate*. When this happens there are rules which have to be applied to decide who gets what. A surviving spouse does NOT automatically get everything; the distribution depends on how much you own at your death and who survives you. First, all debts and funeral expenses are paid. Then the balance will be known. This is called the *net estate*. If the net estate is under £25,000 – the surviving spouse gets it all, no matter who else is around. He/she also always gets your *personal effects* – the car, the contents of the house, clothing, jewellery. If the estate is over £25,000 and you leave children as well, your spouse will get the first £25,000, plus interest on it at 7% from the date of death to its payment, and a life interest in half the remainder. The children will share the other half of the remainder immediately – unless they are under eighteen, in which case it is held for them until they reach that age. Where there are no children, but you leave surviving parents, your spouse gets the first £55,000, plus interest on it at 7% as before, and a life interest in half the remainder. The parents get the other half of the remainder immediately. There are similar provisions for surviving brothers, nephews and nieces.

277 Does the spouse ever take the lot?

A. Yes; always if the estate is under £25,000. In other cases if the dead person had no children, brothers or sisters, parents or nephews and nieces.

278 What about the family house? Is this included in the 'property' and does the spouse have any claim to it as such, if his/her name is not on the deeds?

A. The value of the house is taken into account when assessing the total of the *net estate*. There is no right as such to take the house, but as the surviving spouse can take the first £25,000 (or £55,000), it is usual for the house to be appropriated towards that entitlement.

279 I have decided not to leave anything to my wife in my will but to give everything to an old friend. Can she do anything about this?

A. Yes, she can. And so can anyone else, for that matter, who was *dependent* on you during your lifetime. Under the Inheritance (Provision for Family and Dependants) Act 1975, any surviving spouse who has not remarried can apply for provision from your estate. The court has very wide powers to interfere with your will and do justice for the widow. The same sort of decision will be made as on a divorce, with care being taken to see that there is a roof over the widow's head and income to provide for day to day living.

280 Who do you mean by 'anyone else'? I am a *common-law wife*, I suppose, as my man and I have never married but have lived together for many years. He won't make a will. Do these rules about intestacy apply to me?

A. A common-law wife who is dependent on a man now has exactly the same claim on his death as if she had been married. The rules of intestacy do not take your status into account, so you would not benefit if Parliament had not changed the law. Again, the provision which can be made by the court is very wide. And any other person who was dependent can apply, too.

281 Can I claim if the person dies without leaving anything?

A. Of course not! There is an old saying about blood and stones; if the dead person supported you during his life but has nothing left on his death – then there is nothing you can do.

282 You keep mentioning property and estate; do these include money?

A. That's legal jargon for you. *Property* means all the things you own – from furniture and televisions to cars and houses. It does not just refer to bricks and mortar. There is a legal distinction between *real property* – which *is* freehold bricks and mortar – and *personal property*, which is everything else including leasehold houses. But for working out what a person's property consists of at the time of his death, this distinction does not need to be made – at least as far as this section of the book is concerned. *Estate* is just another word for the total property you leave. Yes, it does include money; but do be careful not to leave 'all my money' to someone to whom you intend to leave your property because it can be interpreted as meaning your *cash* but nothing more.

283 How do I find an executor? And what does he do?

A. You *could* ask a bank to be an executor; this would almost certainly mean that your estate would have to pay more costs for administration. Most people appoint their spouses and a child (over eighteen) as executor. Only one is strictly needed, but two makes sure that there is usually at least one person able to cope. Or you could ask a friend to act. A sensible rule of thumb is to ensure that at least one of the executors is younger than you are – for obvious reasons! But do make sure that anyone you want to appoint is willing to act. Sometimes a friend is named as executor without his knowledge and then feels awkward when he finds out after your death, but doesn't want to upset the family by refusing. The executor's job is to collect all the assets, pay all the debts and funeral expenses and tax, and then distribute the remainder according to the will. He can always employ a solicitor to do the donkey work, and all fees and expenses are paid out of the estate and NOT by the executor himself. An executor is not paid for his trouble and time. Sometimes you can appoint your solicitor to be an executor; again, ask him if he wants to act and also if he wants to prepare the will. Incidentally, don't worry about your executor dying after you. *His* executor takes over the job of looking after your property as well. If your executor dies before you, so that you die without one – again don't worry. Your next of kin can apply for a grant of *letters of administration with will annexed*. All will be well.

284 What happens when a person dies – as far as his will is concerned?

A. It is easiest to answer this by explaining what *probate* is. When you make a will and die, the giving effect to that will is achieved by law by *proving* the will in a Probate Registry (a branch of Somerset House). The will is *proved* by producing it with a sworn statement by the executor at the Probate Registry which then issues a Grant of Probate. This is the authority which enables the executors to do their work, and is essential in cases where a house has to be transferred or handed over. Anyone who holds property belonging to the dead person – banks, companies in which he had shares, insurance companies, for example – will need to see a formal document before they will part with what they hold. The grant of probate *is* the proof they need.

285 Is it the same if I don't make a will?

A. Similar, but not the same, because there is no will to prove. The person entitled to do so can apply to the Probate Registry for *letters of administration*.

286 Who can apply?

A. The nearest next of kin – usually the surviving spouse. But children, grandchildren, parents, grandparents may apply if no one with a prior entitlement does so. And a creditor can also seek letters of administration if he thinks that no one will pay him what he is owed! The procedure is marginally more complicated for such an appointment; a form of insurance has to be taken out to ensure that the person does the job properly. The Probate Registry will issue a Grant of Letters of Administration to the applicant – which then has the same force at law as probate and is used for the same purposes.

287 Can anything be done before probate or letters of administration have been granted?

A. It depends. Bank accounts are frozen, houses can't be sold without a Grant. It can be a 'Catch-22' situation because you cannot obtain a grant unless you have paid Capital Transfer Tax (see question 388), and to do this, of course, you need money. So, executors often have to start going through the motions of obtaining a bank account and a loan prior to applying for a Grant.

288 How can I contest my father's will? He always said that he would leave me everything (my mother died some years ago), and I have lived in the house all my life. Now he has left me a few hundred pounds and the rest to a charity.

A. If you were 'dependent' on him, then you may have a claim (as in question 279) under the recent new law. Apart from that, you could only try and upset the will if you could show that there was some irregularity in it. A later will could exist making different provision; or the will could have been made without regard for the proper formalities – only one witness or none; not dated; crossings out or alterations; the witnesses could have been beneficiaries (though that will only prevent them getting anything, not upset the will); or there could have been 'undue influence' – hanky-panky of some sort – ranging from suggesting to the deceased that he ought to make better provision for one person rather than another, to writing the will and holding his hand. This is difficult to prove. And there is nothing to stop a person making any sort of will he likes; simply because you think you ought to have benefited is not in itself a good reason for interfering with the wishes of your father.

289 How can I make sure that my will is not challenged though I am bedridden in hospital?

A. Apart from repeating that there is no way in which you can stop a person from making a claim against your estate if he can show dependence, the best bet is to get your will prepared by a solicitor. The hospital social worker will try and put you in touch with a solicitor who could come to visit you in hospital; or you could get a friend to contact one for you and ask for your instructions to be carried out. Provided that you are in good mental health, you could write out the will yourself and sign it. Then get two nurses – or better still a doctor and a nurse or your solicitor – to witness the signature. It would then be extremely difficult for anyone to claim that you were not of *sound mind* as the doctor could be called to give evidence of your state of mind at the time you made the will.

290 You state making a will avoids trouble. I have only got a few bits of furniture, some cash, and a few pounds in a savings account. Is it really important that I make a will? Won't the cost of probate, and so on, use up all I have?

A. In your case, *probate* may not be necessary, since the relatives can take actual possession of your property immediately, or can arrange for the money in the savings bank (providing it does not exceed £500) to be handed over to the person entitled. Many other bodies will make payments (up to limits) without a Grant – building societies, trade unions, insurance companies, for example. It is still a wise precaution to make a will, however simple, because then the *person entitled* is known and can show that he is identifiable. But if you do not make a will there may be a fight over who gets what. There is nothing like a will dispute to split a family.

291 Can't I 'nominate' savings certificates and money in an account and so avoid will-making?

A. Yes, this can be done, providing you get the appropriate forms from the Post Office and complete them in the right way before you die. There can be few things more infuriating for those who are left behind than to find that the dearly departed has not done some simple thing which would have avoided time, trouble and, above all, expense.

292 One thing that troubles me about wills and probate is the time that is taken before things are finally concluded. One hears of delays taking several years; is there any reason for this sort of delay, and what can one do to cut it down?

A. The various steps are these: obtain probate – that takes about eight weeks or so. Then collect the assets and pay the debts. Asset identification may take a little time if the dead person did not leave everything straight. And, as people often do not expect to die, their affairs can be complicated. The two main sources of delay are in debt paying. The Capital Transfer Tax (see question 388) and outstanding income tax have to be paid. The first is usually fairly clear, at least in small estates; the latter is not so easy to sort out. Tax may still be due or may be repayable. Inland Revenue offices are, through pressure of work, unable to reply to letters quickly; and the Capital Taxes Office is also a slow correspondent. Just working out and dealing with the tax can take several months, unfortunately. Other delays may be caused by: an unexpected dependent turning up with a claim against the estate; litigation outstanding – say, for an accident; the sale of a house – waiting for a buyer may take several months these days; and one can find that there are delays caused by, say, an executor living in another country. Where there is a solicitor dealing with the administration of the estate, you should badger him (within reason) to tell you the causes of the delays. And there is no reason why an interim distribution should not be made in an appropriate case.

293 Can I apply for a grant of probate myself as an executor of my brother's will without using a solicitor?

A. Yes; the Probate Registry has a Personal Applications Department which has an excellent record of sympathetic help for people who are doing it themselves. Fees are payable which are related to the size of the net estate (for addresses see page 206).

294 I have been trying to do a probate application myself but have come up against all sorts of difficulties raised by the probate people because of what they say are alterations in the will. My father made the will, and it was signed and witnessed properly, but he added a line increasing one of the legacies. I know he meant it, and it is obviously his handwriting. Why should this be a problem?

A. Well, *you* may know it is his writing, but how can you expect the Probate Registry to know? And what if the alteration didn't increase a legacy but cut you out of the will? Then you might see it rather differently, mightn't you? Before a will is admitted to probate the court has to be satisfied the document is correct and was what the deceased person signed. Remember one cannot ask him, and so if there is any alteration, crossing out or addition which is not initialled by the testator and the witnesses and dated, it will be presumed – until the contrary be proved – that this was done *after* the will was signed, and so the alterations will have no effect. This means that the witnesses may be asked to make statements about the form of the will when they signed – whether any change had been made, etc. – before probate can be issued. And the same applies to any mark on a will, which may suggest that there was some other document which formed part of, or was incorporated in, the will. So, NEVER use a paper clip to attach anything to a will: put it in a clean envelope and seal it.

295 What do I do to remake a will or to change my wishes?

A. It all depends on the sort of change. If it is a simple one or two lines, you can make a *codicil*, which is an addendum to a will and made in the same way – that is: dated, signed by the person making it, and the signature witnessed by two people (who need not be the same two as on the original). But if the alteration is more complicated, make a new will incorporating your new ideas. Complete this in the formal way (date, signature, two witnesses), and *then* destroy the old will. Don't do it the other way round; the shock of tearing up the old will might kill you off and leave you intestate!

296 Does marriage have any effect on a will?

A. Yes, indeed. It revokes a will: that is, it means that any will made prior to the marriage is invalid for all purposes. The only exception is where a will is prepared in contemplation of marriage – and this is quite unusual these days.

297 What about divorce?

A. Oddly enough, that has no effect at all. Anyone who has been divorced ought to think about his or her will particularly if, for example, one has left property 'to X' (the spouse), because X will automatically be entitled as a beneficiary. But an ex-spouse has *no* entitlement under the rules of intestacy.

298 Is a will a final document?

A. Yes – to the extent that if you are run over the next day, it will be taken as the last expression of your wishes and intentions about what is to happen to your property. But, no – because it can always be altered or updated. The will

that you make when you are first married with young
children is not likely to be the same one that you will make
when you are retired with several grandchildren. It is always
wise to review your will every few years to make sure that it
reflects your wishes, that executors are still alive and in good
health, and that your bequests are in line with inflation and
the value of your property. Remember that values do change
rapidly, and despite increases in Capital Transfer Tax
thresholds you may have a shock – or your family may.

**299 I have no relations at all and no person to whom I would
want to leave my property. What should I do with it?**

A. Apart from giving you the name and address of my
favourite dog! ... you can always leave the property to a
charity. If you have literally no one who can show that they
are related to you in any way and make no other provision,
the money will go to the Crown. Some people are perfectly
content that this should happen and even make specific
directions to that effect. But the usual thing in your case
would be to give it to charity. This has advantages from the
Capital Transfer Tax angle (see question 394), and also,
of course, bestows genuine benefit on the organization. In
order to avoid claims by competing charities with similar
names, it is best to get in touch with your chosen body or
bodies and ask them to send you full details of their correct
name and address. Often you will find that they have a
recommended form of wording which you can insert in the
will which makes sure that the money goes to the right place.

300 Does sex make any difference to inheritance?

A. No; when a death occurs after 1925 males and females
are treated exactly the same for all purposes, and there is no
preference given to eldest sons, or sons over daughters –
except where Arms or Titles are being transferred on death.
For the likes of you and me, sex makes no difference at all.

301 Can you have such a thing as a 'joint will' made and signed, say, by a husband and wife?

A. Yes, you can. This is odd, because you might have thought a will was such a personal document that it would have to be individual and unique. A joint will is *proved* – that is, probate is applied for – on the death of the first testator; then it is *proved* again on the death of the second one. While there is nothing wrong with a joint will, it is much more common for couples to make *mutual wills* – that is, one by each person making identical provision for the other, so as to ensure that the survivor gets everything.

302 My solicitor put a clause in my will saying that my wife had to survive me for thirty days in order to benefit. Why should this be done?

A. It used to be done to save estate duty. Until 1974, if a man died leaving everything to his wife and she died at the same time (say in a crash) or within a short period, estate duty (or death duty) was payable twice on the same money. This caused hardship, as indeed did the paying of duty by widows generally. So, the rule was changed. When Capital Transfer Tax was introduced all gifts between husband and wife – in lifetime or on death – were made free from all Capital Transfer Tax. So a *survivorship clause* (as it is called) is not necessary for tax saving. But it may still be a good idea if you want to ensure that you have some control over the destination of your property. A straight gift to your wife means that the property passes to her as at the date of your death. Should she die with you in a crash or within a few days, the property *you* left her will be *hers*, and will be dealt with under her will. And she might have left it to someone whom you would not wish to receive it. Or if she did not make a will, she would die intestate. As we have seen, the rules of distribution on an intestacy could mean that *her* family could get all *your* money (unless there were children, of course). So, if you insert a clause saying that she must survive you by thirty days or a month (there is no magic in the length of time), and providing you make a suitably worded clause in the will dealing with what is to happen if she *does not* survive, then your in-laws will not automatically get your property if you both die in a crash.

303 Is there any age limit for making a will?

A. In practically all cases you have to be eighteen before you can make a valid will if you live in England and Wales. The only exceptions are servicemen under eighteen who are on *actual military service*. Such wills need not be in writing, or if signed need not be witnessed (they used to be called paybook wills).

304 What is the difference between a 'bequest' and a 'legacy'?

A. There is no real difference nowadays. They are both names for gifts in a will.

305 What happens if I leave something to someone in my will but he dies before I do?

A. If the *someone* is a *child* of yours, the gift is paid to his executor or representative for distribution according to his will. But in the case of any other person who fails to survive you, the gift lapses. The property which comprised the gift is said to *fall into residue* – that is, it forms part of your estate after all individual gifts have been dealt with.

306 I have just heard that one of the people who signed my will as a witness has died. Do I need to make a new will?

A. No; the witness is a vital ingredient to the validity of the will at the time it is made. But once he has signed, a witness ceases to have any part to play. Only if there was any doubt about your signature, or any alteration or crossing out in the will would the witness be contacted. So don't worry.

307 I want my will to be kept private after my death, and I certainly don't want details to be published in the Press. How can I make sure that this happens?

A. You can't. Wills, once proved at the Probate Registry, are public property and are open to inspection by anyone who goes to Somerset House and pays the fee of 25p. And you can obtain a copy for an extra 25p a page. Newspapers obtain details by inspecting the records and see the gross and net values of the estate, and, if the person is a local notable or a national figure, may quote details of gifts made.

308 I know that a witness cannot benefit under a will, but is an executor similarly disqualified?

A. No; executors can and do benefit under wills.

309 Is there any way of registering a will so that it won't be overlooked?

A. You can't register it; but you *can* deposit it at Somerset House or any district Probate Registry for safe custody, either in person, by letter or by someone who is authorized on your behalf. The will must be in a sealed envelope endorsed with details of yourself, the date of the will, and the names and addresses of your executors. A fee of £1 is payable and a Certificate of Deposit issued. On your death, an executor can obtain the will on production of a death certificate and the Certificate of Deposit.

310 If one doesn't go to this length, where should a will be kept?

A. The best thing is to keep all your important papers together. Details of your savings and building society accounts, bank accounts, stocks and shares as well as any other houses or other property should be jotted down and updated and kept with your will. Some people do not like having a will in the house; well, you can ask your bank to safeguard it – they may make a small charge. But be sure to tell someone *which* bank it is with. Legal periodicals are always carrying advertisements asking for details of wills which are believed to exist but which cannot be traced. You may cause a lot of heartache if your family cannot trace your will. And if it cannot be found, then you may well be treated as an intestate with all the consequences.

311 What if my will is destroyed by accident, because the solicitor accidentally throws it out, or it is eaten by the dog, or put in the fire?

A. If there is a copy in existence, or if there is clear evidence available about what the will contained, an application can be made to the Probate Registry for the copy to be admitted to probate, or for details given by oral evidence to be admitted. That is why most sensible solicitors keep copies of wills and make the copies up when the will has been signed and witnessed.

312 Is a grant of probate proof of death as well?

A. Not of itself; usually the probate states the date of death but a certificate of death, or of presumed death, issued by the Registrar General at St Catherine's House, is the only formally acceptable proof of death.

313 What happens if two people die at the same time or in circumstances which make it impossible to show who actually died first?

A. This can happen in plane crashes and in other disasters, and it can be important because the order of death can determine the order of succession to property. So, there is a rule about it. Where no one knows who died first, it is presumed that the eldest died first. There are exceptions to this rule when people die intestate, which is another good reason to make a will.

314 Can a person who is a mental patient make a will?

A. A person must be of full age and of *sound mind* to make a valid will. If medical evidence is available to show that the testator was not of *testamentary capacity* – that is, he didn't know what he was doing – the will is void. Merely because someone is a mental patient, or has had a Receiver appointed by the Court of Protection (see question 365), does not, of itself, mean that he cannot make a will, because he may know precisely what he is doing. So, it can be very important to have medical evidence if a will is produced by a person who has a history of mental trouble – to see if it was made in a lucid interval.

315 I am blind, how do I make a will?

A. In the same way as anyone else – except that it is probably sensible to get a solicitor or someone you can rely on to write it out or type it. Then you sign it, in the same way as you sign any other document, having first had the will read over to you. Your signature is witnessed by two people, and there you are. When the time comes for probate, the court may require an *affidavit* from someone who can say that you did know what was in the will and that it *was* a will you were signing.

142

316 Can someone who cannot write make a will?

A. Yes. The person's wishes are dictated to someone who can write and the will prepared. It is then read over, and the person makes a mark. This is witnessed and additional words are included to say that the will was read over to the testator who understood and approved its contents.

317 What happens when someone dies in my house?

A. First you should tell the doctor who has been attending the person (if that be the case), because he can then certify death. There is no requirement for a doctor who has been regularly attending a patient whose condition might be terminal and saw him within fourteen days to see the body. If the death is sudden, or if no doctor was concerned, a coroner must be informed and an inquest may well be necessary.

318 Are there any other cases where a coroner's inquest is needed?

A. Yes, where the cause of death is unknown, or if violence is suspected, or if death occurred during an operation, or possibly because of an industrial injury.

319 Does the funeral have to wait until the inquest has taken place?

A. Not necessarily. Sometimes a post-mortem examination will reveal the cause of death, and an inquest will not take place. If there is to be an inquest, the coroner can issue an order for burial which allows the body to be released and then prepared for the funeral prior to the inquest actually being concluded. Often the inquest is formally opened and then adjourned for evidence, etc., to be prepared. The funeral takes place when the coroner authorizes the issue of a death certificate. A special certificate is required if the body is to be cremated.

320 Whose job is it to arrange the funeral?

A. There is a list of people: first, the executors; the parents of a dead child; a householder in whose house the body lies; the local authority. If the local authority do it, they can recover the cost from the deceased's estate, or from a person who was under a duty to maintain the person (e.g. spouse, or parent of a child under sixteen).

321 I want to leave my body to a hospital, so that the best use can be made of my bits and pieces. Can I say this in my will, and can I ensure that I an not cremated?

A. Once you are dead, that is it – you have no say in what happens. So, anything you put in your will about your body is not binding on your executors. But you may lawfully ask that any part be used for medical purposes. If you want to be a kidney or eye donor, in particular, it is very important that these wishes are known well in advance by someone who can make arrangements immediately you are dead – or carry a card; because speed is vital if the organs are to be of use. If you say nothing about what is to become of your body, your executors can authorize its medical or anatomical use.

7

EVERYDAY ENQUIRIES

322 I live in a town and do not have a garage for my car. Other people frequently park outside my house, causing me to drive round looking for a parking place, sometimes quite a distance from home. What can I do to ensure that the space outside the house is kept for me?

A. The short answer is, you cannot do anything. A highway is primarily intended for travelling along; the right to stop on it is limited to picking up or dropping passengers or delivering goods. To park on it overnight or for any long period is rather like using it as a garage, and you have no *right* to do this. Stopping on a highway is an obstruction; and if it becomes an *unreasonable* one – because other people cannot pass by, or fire engines are prevented from access to premises, or you cause a hazard – then you are liable to civil action for *nuisance* – as well as criminal proceedings for obstruction. (This is leaving aside the yellow-lining with which one has to comply anyway, of course.) So, you may think that you are being very sensible and public spirited by finding a quiet side road to park in where there are no parking restrictions in evidence, but still find you are prosecuted because you are blocking people from getting in or out of their premises. You have no right to treat the bit of road in front of your house as yours. If, on the other hand, you had a garage or parking space alongside your house and found other people parking in front of it, so blocking your access, then you would have every right to ask the police to take action against the offending motorist. That is all, though.

323 Going along the main street recently I was stunned to see my picture looking at me from a photographer's shop. It was on a sign inviting people to use the man to take pictures at weddings, and so on. Has he any right to make commercial use of my image?

A. Yes. You have no right to privacy as such, and anyone can take pictures of you and publish them in newspapers or magazines or use them for advertising purposes. If the advertising suggests that you are endorsing a product which you are not, then you may have a claim for libel. Using pictures of living people without their permission is, in some cases, contrary to the British Code of Advertising Practice, and you could complain to the Advertising Standards Authority (see page 204).

324 Would this apply to photos of my house?

A. Yes, the principle is the same – you cannot stop people photographing or copying anything that you own. This even applies to people flying over and taking pictures of your property. The right to airspace only goes up as high as one can reasonably need to use it.

325 Can I prevent the Electricity Board from draping wires across my garden?

A. Yes. The Electricity Boards have powers to place an electric line over any ground – *except* a garden, or land covered with buildings. But they can put a line *under* your garden, although they need your consent for new works, and you can ask to be paid; you can object, too. Once the line is erected, they may enter at any time to repair, alter or renew the line.

326 What about cutting my trees or hedges to enable wires to be freed? Can they do that?

146

A. The Electricity Board can give you notice to cut or lop a tree or hedge which is interfering with their wires. If you do not do anything about it, they can do it, although you may seek some compensation. The same principle applies to the roots of trees interfering with underground cables or pipes, but the board cannot enter your land to dig holes without your consent.

327 What is the legal responsibility of schools? My child has been sent home early on a number of occasions, usually because of bad weather or strikes. Can the school just dump children on the street?

A. A teacher is expected to take the same sort of care of a child as a normal parent would. The age of the child is obviously material and so is the activity in which he is taking part. To send a child home early may be negligent if he/she is very small, not because the school has any obligation to keep the child until its parent appears, but because there has been an un-notified change in the timetable. Thus, the school could send a circular to each parent saying that the hours would be changed or that school dinners would not be provided any more. Then parents would be expected to make what arrangements they thought necessary to ensure that the child was met or shown how to get home.

328 Can you explain to me what happens when a company goes bankrupt?

A. First of all, let us get the labels right. When money runs out, an *individual* goes *bankrupt*, a *limited company* goes into *liquidation*. The legal consequences are similar in many ways, but the practical ones are very different. Insolvency (which is a word covering both bankruptcy and liquidation) happens when an individual cannot pay his bills – whether he is a trader or just an unlucky or thriftless person; or when a limited company is unable to trade. The most usual reason for insolvency is being in debt. When an individual is made bankrupt he is treated as an inferior person – at least financially. He cannot hold property, be a director of a company, or run a business; his bank account is frozen, and many difficulties arise because his affairs are dealt with by a person called a *trustee-in-bankruptcy*. The worst aspect (from the bankrupt's point of view) is that he is liable in theory to the last penny that he owes and will not be discharged until everyone has been paid off. The rules have been relaxed recently, but there is still a continuing responsibility for paying off all creditors. A limited company going into liquidation, however, is in a different category. Only its available assets can be used to pay off the debts. If there are no assets, or huge debts, the chances are that most creditors will whistle for their money. This can cause hardship or loss for ordinary people who have paid money for goods or services to a company which fails and has no assets available.

329 How can someone apparently go out of business and yet open up again at the same place, without any liability for what he was previously doing?

A. This, again, depends on the status of the *person* carrying on the business. An individual or a partner is liable for all his debts for all time. He cannot limit or evade his *liability*. (He may evade *payment* – but that is a different matter altogether to liability). So, if Bill Thomas & Co. – your local butcher – stops trading, the proprietor (and any partners he may have) are personally liable for all debts. So he cannot open up again without still carrying the responsibility for the debts incurred in the past. That is one reason why solicitors and accountants, for example, are not allowed to form themselves into limited companies. A limited company (which you can recognize because it always has the word *Limited* in its name) is treated as a separate legal entity. So Bill Thomas & Co. Limited (still your local butcher, but a different legal creature altogether from the one up the page) can go into liquidation and open up again at the same premises with
148

the same personnel and call itself Bill Thomas & Co. (1979) Limited. That is a new legal creature and is not in any way connected or related to the previous one. It seems crazy, I know, but if one started to prevent companies from being set up by people who had been involved with one that had gone out of business in the past, there could be great unfairness. There is a move to prevent people who have been directors of two companies that have gone bust from being directors again; but there is no definite prohibition.

330 Is there any way in which I can find out where a company carries on business or who is controlling it?

A. Be careful how you use the word *company* – because it is used to describe both a small partnership, for instance, as well as a limited company. If two or more people carry on business in partnership (or if one person carries on business) under a name which is not the actual name of the individuals concerned, then details must be registered at the Companies Registry under the Registration of Business Names Act 1916. This requires the name and address of each person who is a partner and their nationality as well as the trading name, of course. So if Bill Thomas & Co. consists of me alone, no registration is necessary; but the same name with one or more partners will mean all their names will have to be set out and the details registered. You have a right to inspect details of any registered business name (see page 205).

331 What about limited companies?

A. These have to be registered and details lodged of all people who are directors, of the secretary, the registered office and the shareholders. From the files at Companies House (see page 205) you can find out a considerable amount of information about just who owns what and whether a company is part of a group or is a subsidiary.

149

332 What is the registered office?

A. It is the address at which notices and summonses must be served upon the company. It is the formal address, if you like, although it is frequently NOT the place where the company actually carries on its business, but a solicitors' or accountants' office. This address is needed if ever you have to take a limited company to court because all papers have to be served on it at that registered office.

333 A friend at work has asked me to be a guarantor for a hire-purchase agreement. I am not sure about agreeing. Should I?

A. It is up to you to decide, depending on many things – how long you have known the friend, whether he/she has a house, a steady job, savings, and so on. You see, by being a guarantor you are laying yourself wide open to a claim by the hire-purchase company if the friend does not pay what is owing. While you will have a claim against him/her for any sums you have to pay as guarantor, it could be a long and tedious struggle to get it; that is why the h.p. firm *wants* a guarantor – to save it from expense if the person doesn't make his commitments. Lots of people find that they are let down by so-called friends who default on agreements. So, think very hard about it and do not be afraid to say no.

334 I am fed up with people sitting on my front garden wall, which is immediately next to a bus stop. They pick flowers from the garden and throw their litter in too. Can I put barbed wire along the top of the wall?

A. Not unless you want to get into trouble with the local council. Under the Highways Act it is an offence to keep barbed wire adjacent to a public highway if the council has served a notice telling you to take it down. So that is not a good idea. You could grow a stout hedge, providing you ensured that it did not overhang the pavement.

150

335 While I was arranging to hire a colour television I was asked to pay a deposit of several months' instalments. I agreed to this and produced a credit card to settle the amount. The trader said that he could not accept this as a method of payment because he had to have cash. Is this right?

A. Oddly enough, yes. The rules about hiring do state that any *deposit* must be by cash or cheque. As this form of trading is used as one of the ways in which to try and regulate the economy, I suppose there is some justification for making people put down hard cash for a deposit rather than using credit facilities which would defeat the object of having the deposit. But as the trader is paid straightaway by the credit card company the money is in his hands almost as quickly as if he had been paid by cheque.

336 If a person is dealt with by the criminal courts for assault can he then be sued for compensation by the injured victim in the civil courts?

A. Unless the assailant pleads guilty – in which case you *can* sue – if he goes to the criminal courts and is either convicted or acquitted after a contest, he cannot be sued. Your remedy, I suppose, would be to ask the court which convicts him to make a compensation order.

337 I was unable to go on a holiday that I had booked because of illness. Two things arose: first I could not get back the deposit I had paid, because the company said it was not their policy to repay money; secondly, I had taken out what I thought was an insurance policy to cover me, but they would not pay out either. Is there no justice is this world?

A. Very little! The first point you raise is a good example of a true legal deposit (see question 165). The company made it a term of the contract that you *had* to pay a proportion of the cost as a condition of making a booking. And they also said that if you broke the contract you would lose the deposit. Well, you did, and you did! So they are dealing perfectly fairly. The second point is more difficult. It is very important when you apply for holiday insurance that you understand what you are doing. All insurance contracts require you to make full disclosure of *material facts* (see question 363), which means things like previous illnesses, pre-existing medical conditions, for *everyone* going on the holiday. So, if Gran has a wooden leg, or you had a heart attack ten years ago, or Tracey is an asthma sufferer, you must tell the insurer, otherwise they can deny the claim because of non-disclosure. So I suspect that the insurer to whom you entrusted your premium has discovered some medical fact hidden away somewhere and is using that to avoid paying you.

338 I want to change my surname, but my husband is unhappy about it and says it will cause all sorts of problems with banks and the Social Security. What can I do?

A. A surname is a label – no more, and no less – for an individual and you can change it in different ways. The simplest is just to say that you want to be called Smith from now on instead of Jones. Tell everyone, and that is that. But banks and institutions like to have something in writing, so you could make a simple *statutory declaration* setting out your new name and stating that you wish to abandon the old surname. You must have your signature attested by a solicitor who will charge you £1 for making a declaration. Or you could get him to deal with the whole thing for you. In either of these cases you do not need anyone's consent or approval. The production of the statutory declaration will be sufficient for most purposes – for banks, building societies, the Land Registry, the D.H.S.S. and the Passport Office. If you want to go all formal and pay quite a lot of money, you can do a *deed poll*, which is a document to which you need to annex your birth and marriage certificates (and any decree absolute), advertise in the *London Gazette* and enrol in the High Court. And you need your husband's consent! You will almost certainly need a solicitor to do this for you – and his costs will be on top of the fees you have to pay for certificates, enrolment, and so on.

339 Is this procedure the same for children?

A. For anyone under eighteen, the consent of the father is needed for deed poll. If you are divorced and want to change the surname of your children, you will find difficulties because there have been recent cases where the divorce court has refused to allow a child's name to be changed.

340 My husband and I have a joint bank account on which either of us can draw cheques. What happens if either of us dies?

A. You will be treated as *joint-tenants* (which has nothing to do with housing!), which means that the survivor takes the lot. So, with a joint bank account you can go on drawing money if your husband dies because what is left in the account belongs to you; it became yours by survivorship the moment your husband died and was not dependent on any grant of probate or the will which he might have left. The same principle applies to other shared accounts – like building society and savings bank accounts, as well as stocks and shares. There is just one thing you should look out for – an unexpected consequence. Let me illustrate with a real life example. A widower re-married late in life and put his house into the joint names of himself and his new wife – as *joint-tenants*. A few years later he became an invalid and sold the house; the money was put into an account at a building society – in joint names. The couple rented a flat. The old gentleman then made a will leaving everything to his wife for her lifetime, and then to his children, with a few little gifts to his grandchildren. He died. As nothing happened about the gifts being paid to the grandchildren, one of his sons wrote to the stepmother asking what was wrong. A letter came back from the solicitors saying that the only asset the old man had was his joint-share in the building society, and that because of the joint-tenancy it passed instantly on his death to his widow; and she was not going to make any of the money available to anyone. This was quite contrary to what he would have wanted; and his generosity and desire to help his new wife misfired. He could not have changed it all before he died, because his wife would have had to agree. But he could have *severed* the joint-tenancy, which would have salvaged half. If he had taken full advice about his affairs when he made his will, his solicitor should have spotted the trap.

341 What rights do I have when I use a car-park?

A. It all depends on the terms and conditions (if any) which the car-park owner imposes. Almost certainly there is no contract as such: you simply pay your money to park your car, and the person owning the park doesn't have to take much care of it as he is not even a *bailee* unless you hand over the keys. So, your *right* is to drive on to the site and leave your car, and then to go back later and collect it. If it has been stolen or damaged, you would have no remedy against the car-park firm unless you could show that the employees had been negligent; and they may well impose conditions by a notice in which their liability for negligence may be limited or avoided altogether. In this case, you would be able to challenge the reasonableness of the words in the notice – even though there was no contract.

342 What is the difference between an estimate and a quotation?

A. An estimate is what it sounds like – an approximate indication of what the final charge will be. So, it may vary by a reasonable factor – say 10% – either way, possibly more. But if the final bill is very much more, then you can argue

154

that you should not pay anything over the original estimate, plus a bit. A quotation is *the price* at which the job will be done, no more, no less. And it is reasonable for a customer to treat that as the final price – inclusive of V.A.T. A trader giving an estimate ought to indicate whether or not V.A.T. is included.

343 Last summer a man came to the house and bought a cooker I had advertised. He paid the agreed price and said he would call back, but has never done so; it must be a year ago now. The cooker gets in the way. What can I do?

A. Technically nothing, because the cooker does not belong to you since the ownership passed as soon as he paid you for it. Until recently you would have had to hold it for him. But the law has now been changed to help people in your position. Section 12 of the Torts (Interference with Goods) Act 1977 allows a *bailee* who cannot trace the owner of goods to sell them; you have to account to the true owner for any profit, of course, so that you must be able to pay him the money if and when he turns up. Alternatively you could apply to the court for an order for sale – which would probably be a sensible thing to do if the goods were valuable. Note also that this Act applies to anyone, not simply to traders (see question 199).

344 I bought some goods which were advertised in a national magazine. The seller lived in Yorkshire, and it was agreed between us that he would put them on a door-to-door carrier service, for which I paid the carriage charge. When they arrived they were in a terrible state, and I refused to accept delivery. The seller said that it was nothing to do with him as they had become my property as soon as they went on to the lorry. I am sure this isn't right – but can I do anything?

A. The Sale of Goods Act is clear on this point: delivery to a carrier by the seller is delivery to the buyer, and so the ownership and the risk passes too. Therefore, if the goods are damaged in transit, they are *your* goods and your problem. The only hope you have is to argue that the contract of carriage which the seller made is not a reasonable one because the terms and conditions are unfair, for example, in that they require complaints to be made within a very short time limit or restrict liability to a small sum. But in your case you agreed to the carrier, and so you would be presumed to have known what you were up to, and the only claim that you could make would be to show that the *carrier* was negligent and had caused the damage.

345 What obligations do I have when I sell my car privately?

A. First to ensure that you describe it correctly; if you do not, the buyer can claim his money back from you under the Sale of Goods Act. Secondly, to make sure that it is roadworthy, because it is a criminal offence to sell a car which is not.

346 Near where I live is a garage. In addition to servicing and repairing cars it also sells petrol, and it has recently started opening all night. Previously it was only open during the day and early evening. The floodlights are left on, and there is a lot of noise during the night with doors banging and cars revving up. Is this sort of thing legal, and can I and my neighbours do anything about it?

A. Noise is one form of environmental pollution; it may also be a *nuisance*. Recent new laws have increased the powers of local authorities to try and stop unnecessary noise, either by taking the offender to the magistrates court, or by obtaining an *injunction*. For the noise to be a nuisance, however, it must be something which is unreasonable or which arises from a change in circumstances. So, if the garage had always been open for twenty-four hours a day, or the noise had always happened, it would be very difficult to establish that anyone had been adversely affected by it; moving to live next to a noise which you don't like doesn't give you any right to complain about it.

347 My neighbour has a large dog which comes through my hedge and messes up my garden; it also frightens my grandchildren. I have tried to get the owner to be reasonable, but he just laughs and says the dog is quite harmless. Can I stop it coming into my garden?

A. The owner is not liable if the dog trespasses on its own; but should the owner deliberately send the dog through the hedge, he would make himself liable to you. Cats don't give rise to any liability at all.

348 Would your answer be different if the animal were different?

A. Yes: cattle, horses, sheep, goats, pigs and poultry are all animals which give rise to a liability for trespass if they stray on to your land. The owner – or the person in physical charge of the creature – is under a responsibility to ensure that there is no trespass and no damage done while it is under his care.

349 What can be done, though, without getting involved in legal complications?

A. You could move house . . . or put up a strong fence or hedge. There is nothing to stop you doing this – unless the deeds of your house contain any restriction on putting up fences.

350 I sent some velvet curtains to the cleaners'; when they came back they were stained and torn. I saw the manager who

told me that he couldn't help me because the work had been done by another company. He had sub-contracted it out, and he suggested that I raised my complaint with that firm. Is this what I have to do?

A. If you did not know about the sub-contracting, or if you did not agree to it – the cleaning company is liable to you. The law is quite clear about this; but problems can arise where the small print allows sub-contracting to happen but you don't realize it. So it all depends on what steps the trader took to tell you. If he did nothing at all, he is fully liable to you. If there was a notice or written contract terms stating that there might be sub-contracting, then your claim is against the sub-contractor unless you can show that the cleaner was negligent by using an inefficient sub-contractor. Another snag is that there might have been a term saying that the trader wasn't liable for any loss which was caused by his own negligence – or that of any one else. The best answer, if you want to avoid going to court each week, is to use a cleaner which belongs to a trade association.

351 I went to buy a pound of sausages and proffered a £5 note. The butcher said that he hadn't any change and demanded the correct money. I hadn't got it – so there was stalemate. Surely one can expect to be given change when out shopping?

A. Although one does expect change, and most traders will willingly give it, the law is that you should tender the correct amount of the price in legal currency. You have no right to insist on change, and technically the trader can refuse to part with the goods you have bought until you do have the right money.

352 Just what is legal currency?

A. The coins made by the Mint – cupro-nickel ('silver') coins up to 10p in value can be tendered for payment up to £5;

bronze coins, for payment up to 20p. Bank of England notes are legal tender, but Scottish bank notes are *not* legal tender, although they are generally accepted by banks along with other *foreign* money.

353 The rental agreement for my televison set says that it is rented for a minimum period of three years and then by the year. When I thought about buying my own TV I enquired at the rental company, and they said they would take the rented set back providing I paid all the money still due for the first three years! This seems that they are having it both ways; have I any right to cancel without having to pay this penalty?

A. At the moment the TV rental company can insist on your doing what the agreement says. In other words, if you go into an arrangement with your eyes open, you cannot complain about it afterwards – it is the old business of knowing and understanding what you sign. If your signature is on the agreement – tough. But there is a change on the way to allow people who have private rental agreements to end them after eighteen months by giving notice of three months or one instalment period, whichever is the less (Consumer Credit Act). It is important to note that this does *not* extend to rentals for business purposes, so that if you hire a telephone answering machine you will probably not be protected.

354 I recently found some money in a bank – on the floor, I mean, not behind the cashier's plate glass! I told the manager who thanked me, took the money and said that it would help reduce the bank's deficit. Surely this money belongs to me?

A. Why should it? It belongs to the true owner, to whom you are responsible for it. It does not belong to the bank either; but as it was found on their premises they may have a marginally better claim to it. In fact, one just does not know what the answer is to the question. What is needed is a modern decision of the courts to determine which of several competing claimants should be entitled in the absence of the true owner. So, why not get the bank to agree to finance a legal case ... ?

355 What would happen if the true owner had simply abandoned the money or thrown it away deliberately?

A. I wish he had waited for me to get there! Where abandonment takes place, the goods belong to the first finder. It may be difficult to distinguish accidental loss from a deliberate giving up of ownership, because unless you were there when the true owner did what he did, you have no way of knowing his intention. Just because you find, say, a ring on the beach doesn't mean that the owner has abandoned it; indeed, probably the very opposite. He just gave up looking for it after hours of fruitless search.

356 Local children keep hitting their cricket balls into the garden. Apart from the risk to my windows, it is very irritating. So I have told them that the next time a ball comes into the garden I shall keep it. Now I have been visited by the police who have warned me that I can't do this, and that I might be prosecuted for theft. Is this right?

A. This is a very odd business. The person who throws the ball over the wall has no right to enter your land to collect it; you have no obligation to go and look for the ball or hand it back. So, if you do nothing and refuse to let the kids come into the garden – that is it. Stalemate. But if you take possession of the ball you take on obligations and must allow the true owner to have it back. So, do nothing and you are in the clear; pick the ball up and you might indeed be guilty of theft if you refuse to hand it back, as well as having little defence to a civil claim for delivery of the ball.

160

357 I am owed money by someone. Several years have gone by since the loan was made, and I haven't received any payment or even an acknowledgment from him. He is still alive and well and working, but I should like to know where I stand.

A. There is a limit for the right to enforce a contract debt. This is six years from the date of the original loan or from the last time the debtor made any acknowledgment of his indebtedness. So, you had better watch out that you don't find yourself *statute-barred* – which would enable the man to avoid payment completely.

358 Can one pick blackberries growing in the country without breaking the law?

A. As long as they are growing wild, you can pick mushrooms, flowers, fruit or foliage without being guilty of theft. You cannot take the whole plant, roots and all, and there are protected species of wild plant which you must not pick. But, that apart, you do not break the criminal law. You may still be interfering with the ownership rights of the person upon whose land the wild plant grows and may be asked to leave the land without the fruit or berries you have picked by the owner or his representative. *Trespass* is a civil wrong which entitles the landowner to claim damages.

359 I have had a letter from the Electricity Board saying that there has been a fault in my meter, and I have not paid enough for the electricity supplied to the house. Surely that is their problem? I have always paid on the nail whenever I have had a bill.

A. In most cases this would be so; if the mistake were made by any other trader who accepted your payment in satisfaction of the bill, the loss would fall on him, and he would not be able to use his own mistake as a good reason to extract more money from you. But where the service is being supplied under an Act of Parliament, this rule (called *estoppel*

161

by lawyers) doesn't apply, and so the board can send a bill for more money even though the mistake was their own.

360 There was a small advertisement in the local paper offering an unwanted wedding present of some cutlery. As I am just about to get married and setting up home, I thought it might be a useful purchase. When I went to the address the person selling seemed to me to be much too slick to be a private seller, so I asked – half-jokingly – if he was always doing this sort of thing. He became very abusive, and the upshot was that I left without buying. Is there any way in which one can tell if a person is a trader?

A. It can be very difficult to identify genuine adverts, and many less respectable traders will use bogus private ads to lure people into buying what are often shoddy goods; then when things go wrong they claim to be just ordinary private sellers with no liability. The law was changed in 1977 in an attempt, if not to stop the practice, at least to indicate to the public that there *was* a business being carried on. Now a person must not advertise goods for sale unless the advert makes it clear whether the sale is in the course of a business. A glance down any small ads column will show that despite this law people are still doing the bogus advertisement stunt. The Trading Standards department will try to enforce the law in a case where you have been taken in.

361 How does one prove that one was born? My parents did not register my birth, and it is very difficult for me when dealing with pension funds and retirement rights. I believe that I am fifty-eight; both my parents are dead and I have no close relatives.

A. The only way to deal with this is to try and get what evidence you can to support your belief. For instance, you may have been paying National Insurance contributions since they started and the old Workman's Compensation

162

payments before that – so there may well be a record of the date you started work on the D.H.S.S. files. Your previous employers may be able to show when you started work, so you may be able to trace it all back to the first job; the Services, too, may have records. Try the Regimental Association if you were in the Army, or the Ministry of Defence records for the arm of the forces you were in. Schools usually destroy records after a few years, but you might have been in a school magazine or something similar which would still exist and indicate roughly how old you were. Baptism records also exist in some cases, and there may have been some record made in a family Bible or other document. Then you can put all the information which you can gather into a statement which can be attested by a solicitor as a *statutory declaration*. This may well go a long way to satisfying people that you are the age you claim to be.

362 Can I make tape recordings of radio programmes and records?

A. There are two things to be considered here. First the *recording* of the music or programme; secondly, the *performance* of what you have recorded. Recording is a breach of the copyright of the person who *made* the programme (the BBC, or independent radio station, for example) or, in the case of a record, the company which made it, whose name is on the label. You can obtain an Amateur Recording Licence for £1.72½ a year which allows you to record the music on records issued by companies which belong to the Mechanical Copyright Protection Society Ltd (see page 206). Having a licence lets you record and play back for your private use. but it *only* covers you playing records which *you* have bought – so you cannot tape from the radio or television – or even from presents! And it only covers companies which belong to the Society; many do not, and you ought to apply to any record company directly for permission. The *performance* is a breach of the copyright of the artist who took part or who recorded the music. The Performing Rights Society (see page 206) looks after the interests of artists and collects royalties for performances which are divided among all artists. The Society allows you to play records in your own home without a licence; but the moment you open the front door, or if you play music (whether on a record or from a radio, concert or recital) in public, you need a Public Performance licence. So, watch out, because the P.R.S. has staff who check in shops and other public places and expect offenders to apply for an immediate licence. It is only fair to the chap who made the record, after all.

363 How is it that insurance companies can disclaim their liability after one has paid a premium for years?

A. This is not an easy question to answer. You have to look at the basis of the relationship between you and the insurance company. When you want to take out an insurance policy, you know a great deal more about whatever it is you want covered than the company does. So you have an obligation to tell the company as much as possible before the policy is issued so that it can decide the amount of risk it is taking on, and fit the premium accordingly. What you have to tell are called *material facts*. The acid test of a material fact is what a prudent insurer would want to know about a risk to be covered, NOT what a reasonable man might think ought to be disclosed. And insurers sometimes don't help by putting general questions in a proposal form, such as 'Is there anything else you want to tell us?' which is meant to be a sweeping-up question to allow you to reveal your past history, criminal records, anything, in fact, which the insurer thinks afterwards you should have told him. And your duty extends to informing the insurer of any changed circumstances when you renew an annual policy. Therefore if you do not disclose a material fact, they disclaim liability.

364 I live alone and I have a house contents insurance policy for my furniture and other personal effects. I shall shortly be

having someone to live with me. Should I tell the insurance company?

A. Yes, indeed. And you should make quite certain that your friend's belongings are separately listed as well. Because if you do not do so, they will NOT be insured under your policy – because they are NOT your property.

365 Can you tell me what the Court of Protection does?

A. It is a branch of the Law Courts which deals with the affairs of people who are mentally handicapped and so cannot cope with things themselves. If there is medical evidence which shows that a person is unable to look after his personal matters – house, business, investments, as well as physically looking after himself – an application can be made for the appointment of a *Receiver*. This is usually a close relative (though it may be an accountant) and he has to give details of the person's income and property to the court. If an order is made for the Receiver to act, he receives money, deals with property and houses and generally looks after the affairs of the mental patient until he recovers or dies. Each year the Receiver has to account to the Court of Protection showing what has been spent and received, and he always has to ask the Court for directions about selling property or stocks and shares.

8

TAXATION

366 I don't understand about V.A.T. – and whether I should apply to be a registered trader. Can one choose when one joins?

A. You have to conform to rules which are laid down about registration. It is not a matter of choice at all. Each quarter you must look at your *turnover* – that is, your gross take in your shop or trade. Did it exceed £3500 for the last quarter, £6000 for the last two, £8500 for the last three, or £10,000 for the last year? If the answer to any of these four questions is yes, you must notify the local Customs and Excise V.A.T. office. Then they take over and send you information about registration, and so on.

367 How can I find out how the V.A.T. system works?

A. The Customs and Excise publish free information Notices; No. 700 and No. 701 contain a general guide and give the scope and coverage of the tax. V.A.T. registered traders also receive a regular up-dating pamphlet called *V.A.T. News*, which sets out alterations and amendments in the rate of tax and the scope of things affected by it, as well as giving information about court decisions on V.A.T.

368 Is it right that V.A.T. can be charged on postage and packing?

A. Yes, it is. And on other expenses which the trader pays out, too. It even extends to other expenses. If I, as a V.A.T. trader, buy your railway ticket for you because we are travelling together on business, I will include the fare in my bill to you. And I will add V.A.T. because the purchase of the ticket by me was the supply of a service to you. Some companies state that they will not pay V.A.T. on such items. There is no basis in law for their refusal, and you can quite properly insist on it being paid.

369 But surely postage stamps and fares are exempt from V.A.T. How can you possibly charge the tax on them?

A. I am not charging V.A.T. on the stamps or tickets *themselves*, but as an incidental to the service which I have supplied in buying them.

370 I am about to buy a newly-built house. Will I be charged V.A.T. on it or on the land upon which it is built?

A. Let's break it down into the components. The *land* is exempt from V.A.T. The construction of the house is *zero-rated*. This means that the builder can reclaim from the Customs the V.A.T. which he will have had to pay on the bricks and other (*standard-rated*) materials which he bought to build the house. So no tax is payable.

371 What about an extension to the house? Is this taxable?

A. There can be difficulties here; you have to distinguish between construction, repair or alteration. If the extension is new work, then it is zero-rated. But if what is being done is repaired – because the garage roof gave way (or the house roof, for that matter) under the weight of snow, the work by the builder will be standard-rated. And if you buy materials yourself to do the work, that will be standard-rated too.

372 I understand that do-it-yourself housebuilding is outside tax. Is this right?

A. No, it is not right. All the materials you use will be standard-rated for V.A.T., and you will have to pay it on top of the cost in the usual way. BUT at the end of the job you will be able to reclaim the tax charged on certain goods and materials – see Notice No. 719, which deals specially with your problem. But the scheme does not extend to the conversion, reconstruction or alteration of any existing building – so the materials used in any work you do on your house once it is finished will be charged at the standard rate, but will be outside the refund provisions.

373 Can you settle an argument about ice-cream and V.A.T.? Is it chargeable or not on ice-creams bought in a shop to take away?

A. Well, as far as ice-creams are concerned, an anomaly has now been removed. All ice-cream, sweets, drinks and crisps are standard-rated in all circumstances. So it doesn't matter if you take it away or eat it in the shop.

374 Do I have to pay V.A.T. on a service charge?

A. Yes.

375 I am a V.A.T.-registered trader. Can you answer two questions for me? First, if I buy a car, can I claim back the V.A.T.; secondly, can I apply to be de-registered?

A. First part first; no, you cannot set off the V.A.T. on a car which you buy for your business. The V.A.T. is a *non-deductable input tax*. Secondly, if your turnover drops to £8500 or less each year for two years running, you can ask for your registration to be cancelled.

168

376 I hear that the Customs and Excise will now allow bad debts to be off-set so that the tax paid can be reclaimed. Is this so?

A. It was high time this unfairness was corrected, and in 1978 a start was made. You can now get relief for V.A.T. lost on non-payment of a bad debt in limited circumstances. The main proviso (which is also the bad news) is that the debtor must have become *formally insolvent* – that is, have been made *bankrupt* if an individual, or been put into a creditors' *liquidation* or compulsory liquidation. So the simple default, or non-payment followed by a court judgment will NOT be sufficient for the V.A.T. to be reclaimed. It does seem illogical that the Inland Revenue will treat these situations as bad debts available as expense against income tax but the Customs won't. But then logic doesn't appear to enter into taxation, does it?

377 Why is income tax treated as something which a husband has to pay and deal with?

A. History, that's all. In fact, changes have been made recently to enable women to be treated more fairly – but there is still some way to go. Husbands and wives can now be separately *taxed* as well as separately assessed. Separate taxation means that you are each treated as single people with the allowance and reliefs appropriate to you as such. If you both earn a lot or if one of you earns a great deal more than the other, there can be quite an advantage in separate taxation because the overall tax bill can be reduced, at least for income tax on earnings. For investment income taxation, the wife's is still treated as being the husband's even after election for separate taxation; so the sums have to be done with great care to ensure that separate taxation is the best thing for you both.

378 Why do tax rebates get sent to my husband although I pay tax on my own account?

A. Because you have not elected to be separately *taxed*. You may well be separately assessed because that makes the division of tax more straightforward; but he still remains technically liable to pay the tax – and to receive the rebates. The law has now been changed in part to provide that P.A.Y.E. rebates should go direct to the wife.

379 My husband died some months ago. He was a pensioner, and I thought that his tax was all worked out. Now I have had a demand from the Inland Revenue to pay some outstanding money. Why do they come to me and do I have to pay?

A. If the income which you and your husband had was being treated as his for tax purposes, on his death the Revenue can split the assessment between his income and yours. You are then taxed on your bit. If insufficient tax had been paid, this demand may result. Otherwise the people who have to pay the tax on a dead person's income are the *personal representatives*. In many cases, of course, the surviving spouse *is* a personal representative and so receives the tax demand in that capacity and not personally. I recognize that if you are doing the paying it doesn't really matter which hat you are wearing.

380 My wife and I have separated. There is no divorce and no formal agreement. How are we treated for tax purposes?

A. First of all you should tell your tax office (or offices if you both work), so long as the separation is permanent. If you pay money to your wife on a voluntary basis you are treated as though you were still living together. No deduction of tax is made from the payments; you are still given the married man's tax allowance; your wife doesn't have to pay tax on the money she receives from you. This means that you are not getting the full advantages of the tax situation which now exists.

381 How can I do this without having to go to court?

A. By making a written separation agreement in which you set out the agreed financial situation. You should split the money between your wife and any children, and when you make the payments you deduct tax at the standard rate. So, if you pay a total of £200 a month, you deduct tax at 30% (the present standard rate) and pay over £140. You have to tell your wife that this has been done and give her a certificate of deduction of tax – Form R185. You then hang on to the tax deducted and reduce the tax that you actually pay. If you pay higher rate tax you may get a further reduction.

382 Is this situation different if a court order is made?

A. Basically it is the same, but there are slightly different rules about deduction of tax. The amount of money paid is material: up to £21 per week for a wife and £12 per child are paid *without* deduction of tax. (These are called *small payments*.) Your income tax will be adjusted to take this into account so that you don't end up worse off – tax-wise, that is.

383 What does my wife do?

A. She receives the payments from you. If you are making *small payments*, she will be assessed on her total income at the end of the year – and may have to pay some tax. Usually she doesn't, because the small payments are geared to the personal allowances. If you are paying larger sums and deducting tax, she will tell the Inland Revenue the gross amount (the full amout including the deducted tax), and her income is then worked out. Account is taken of the tax you have deducted. In many cases a refund will be due to her for some of the tax you have deducted. She should claim from the Inland Revenue.

384 Are children treated the same?

A. Money paid to children will be treated as their income.
So they can receive up to the personal allowance without
having to pay tax. So, if tax is deducted from payments to a
child, a repayment claim can be made on his behalf.

385 Who gets allowances following a separation?

A. In the year you part, the husband gets the married man's
allowance for the whole year; the wife gets earned income
allowance up to that date, then the single person's allowance
thereafter. In later years, the husband gets the single person's
allowance, and so does the wife. The husband can claim the
married man's allowance until a decree absolute. The wife
can claim the additional personal allowance if the children
are living with her after decree absolute. The Inland Revenue
have produced booklets (see page 209) on this which are a
help in trying to unravel the tax situation.

**386 I own a house in which I live. I am about to marry a man
who also owns a house. I expect we shall end up living in his
house, and I shall then think about selling my own. What will
be the Capital Gains Tax situation then?**

A. A husband and wife are treated as one for most Capital
Gains Tax (C.G.T.) purposes, so they can only own one main
house free of the tax. So, you will have to decide which *is*
your main residence; the other one will be subject to C.G.T.
when you sell it. One possible way out is to allow a dependent
relative to live in it; this gives rise to an exemption.

**387 My husband, who owned the house solely, died recently.
His executors sold it (with my full consent), and are making
the proceeds available to me. Do I have to pay C.G.T.?**
172

A. If you lived in the house with your husband, then the answer is no. There is an exemption for this case. And the same would apply if your husband's will had created a trust in which you were a beneficiary allowed to go on living in the house.

388 What is Capital Transfer Tax (C.T.T.)?

A. It is a tax introduced to replace estate duty (or death duty). It also extends to gifts made in a person's lifetime. In theory, it is an almost perfect form of tax, because no one can avoid it, as they could estate duty, by making distributions in life and then making sure that they lived for a given number of years. There have been a substantial number of concessions and exemptions, however, which make its effect less harsh.

389 How does it work?

A. Everything that you own is notionally property which is subject to C.C.T. Anything you give away in your lifetime accumulates. No tax is payable on the first £25,000 of your running total, but tax starts on anything over that. Death is treated as a gift of everything. You should tell the Inland Revenue about gifts you make in your lifetime, on a special C5 form available from the Capital Taxes Office (see page 204). On death, your personal representatives have to make disclosure.

390 Are there any important exemptions?

A. Yes, there are. The first and by far the most important is that all gifts between husband and wife during their lives or on death are completely free from C.T.T. The old injustice that widows had to raise money to pay death duties has been ended. You can give away up to £100 to any number of people in any tax year; give wedding presents of differing amounts depending on your relationship to the couple; and gifts up to £2000 in total, which are not tax free for any other reason. And certain maintenance payments are also exempt.

391 How can one reduce one's C.T.T. liability?

A. As far as possible try to keep as much as you can within a family. It is wise for a husband and wife to split their assets – house, contents, stocks, shares, savings – fifty-fifty, as near as you can, and hold as tenants-in-common (see question 119). This means that the same total is available, but being halved the tax rate applicable to each is lower. For instance, as £100,000 is taxed at 45 %, the tax bill = £45,000; but split it into two lots of £50,000 and the tax rate is 25 % – the total tax bill is £25,000. You would do well to get professional advice from a solicitor or accountant on this. It could be money well spent.

392 Is there no reduction for life-time gifts like the old rules for estate duty?

A. There is a lower rate for lifetime gifts providing the giver lives for at least three years. This is tapered (as the tax rate is in general) and does help a bit. The main snag about C.T.T., from the recipient's point of view, is that the final tax rate will not be known until the giver's death. So there can be a demand for more tax on a gift made some years previously. It is a very complicated tax, except in very straightforward cases, and, unfortunately, you may well need professional help in sorting out what is best.

393 Does C.T.T. apply to the transfer of property between people who are divorced or separated?

A. If you are separated but *still* married – until decree
absolute, that is (see question 49) – the exemption for gifts
between spouses applies, and no C.T.T. is payable on any
rearrangement of your affairs. After you are divorced there
is no exemption unless you can show that there was no
gratuitous intent (which means a desire to give something
away). Thus, if there is a court order transferring the property – house, money or whatever – the Inland Revenue will
treat this as being done *without* gratuitous intent and will
not claim C.T.T. But if you simply give your ex-spouse a
few thousand out of the kindness of your heart, that *will*
attract C.T.T. There is, therefore, a lot to be said for incorporating any sorting out of the matrimonial belongings in a
court order – by consent (see question 64) if possible, and
thereby avoiding C.T.T.

394 If I leave my property to a charity, won't they have to pay C.T.T.?

A. Gifts to charities made at least a year *before* your death
are completely exempt from C.T.T. Gifts on death or within
that last year are exempt up to £100,000. And for a lifetime gift, you could consider taking out an insurance policy
to produce the tax which might be payable if you died in the
following year. You should take professional advice about
this – as you almost certainly would if your property is
worth that sort of figure.

395 In the section on house purchase, you mentioned stamp duty and set out the rates (see question 93). Is it only payable on houses, and isn't it a rather cumbersome way of doing things?

A. Last point first; it is a very cost effective way of gathering
tax. It is cheap to administer, is self-assessing, and is paid on
the nail within a month of the house being bought. There
are dire penalties for being late in paying stamp duty – you

can be directed to pay the duty *again* if you are very late. Apart from house purchase and the grant of leases, stamp duty is payable on the transfer of stocks and shares, certain agreements and trust documents, insurance policies and powers of attorney. It is worth noting, too, that gifts of houses also attract stamp duty in the same way and at the same rates as house purchase (as well, be warned, as potential Capital Transfer Tax depending on the value of the house given away).

9

WHAT TO DO WHEN THINGS GO WRONG

396 What do I do when goods turn out to be defective?

A. First – go back to the shop where you bought them. Ask for the assistant who served you, or the manager. Explain the problem; take your receipt if you have it, or your cheque stub, or credit-card voucher. If this doesn't work, write a letter, keeping a copy, to the shop, setting out your complaint and asking them to rectify what is wrong within a short time – say seven days – and add that if that isn't done, you will treat the goods as having been rejected by you. Secondly, try and get help from an advice centre in your locality (see page 204). Thirdly, if none of these steps results in what you want, find out if the shop or trader belongs to a trade association. If it does, it is well worth contacting the association asking them to intervene, and see what can be done to sort out the mess. Fourthly, if you paid £30 or more and used a credit card, you could contact the appropriate bank and ask for it to help. Remember that the banks which issue credit-cards have a liability to you where there is a breach of contract (see question 206).

397 What if that fails?

A. You may well have to go to law about it. I hesitate before advising anyone to do this, because it is not easy and will take up time and make you worry. But, if all else fails, suing is the only next step to take. The courts exist to try and sort out problems when negotiation fails. If the sum involved is under £200, you can sue in the county court and be reasonably confident that you will not face a huge bill if you lose, because the rules there have been adjusted to encourage people to sort out small claims without using lawyers. That is all very well, but there is no rule saying that a person *cannot* have a lawyer, and many traders do and may thus achieve at least a moral advantage. The procedure is helpfully set out in a booklet called *Small Claims in the County Court* which is available free from any county court. If your claim is over £200, the normal rules about costs apply, and the loser generally has to pay the winner's legal expenses. The county court has an upper limit of £2000, so that any dispute over this sum has to be brought in the High Court. Here the costs can be considerable, and the procedure complicated; the need for professional representation is almost essential. High Court cases take a long time to come to trial, too, unlike the county court, where you can have the dispute heard by a judge within a few months of starting out.

398 How do I get my money if I win a case?

A. Ah, now you are putting your finger on the spot. Winning a case – getting judgment – is the easy bit. Persuading the loser to pay up can be an endless task, if he doesn't want to co-operate. If the loser is a trader in a good way of business, or if he is supported by an insurance company, as he often will be in a motoring case, the winner has only to wait a short time for his money. But an opponent who is an uncertain businessman, or a self-employed person, can play havoc and also make you wonder what justice is all about. It is important to remember that extracting the money is *not* the job of the court. Once you win, it is up to *you* to use any of the ways the rules allow you. But although the court will assist with applications of one kind and another it will not get blood from a stone, especially an unwilling one.

399 What methods are there?

A. Putting in the bailiff (or the sheriff in a High Court case); you pay a fee to the court and the bailiff will see if the debtor has enough goods on which to *levy execution*. If he has, they are seized and sold, and you will get some or all of the judgment debt and the costs – and the fee on issuing the summons to the bailiff. But, if there are no goods, or lots of other creditors, you get nothing, and you lose the fee as well – which can be as much as £15. If the debtor works, you can think about an order to *attach his earnings* which, if made, will mean that his employer will pay regular sums to you. Should you know the debtor's bank account, you could issue a *garnishee* summons – which enables you to grab money due to him from his bank or other debtors of his. If the debtor is self-employed, you could consider making him *bankrupt* if the total due is £200 or more – but this is expensive and not all that certain to get your money for you. Or apply for an *oral examination* at which the man has to come to court and explain what his income, capital, debts and property are. Jolly good, in theory, but often he cannot be served because he is evading service, or he does not turn up, or he does come but is a convincing liar. You end up having paid out more to try and enforce your judgment but are no nearer getting your money. What it all boils down to is this: payment of all judgments requires the co-operation of the person who has to pay. The very fact that you have had to sue and then think about ways of parting him from his money usually means that he will not be willing to help you. So, it can be a dispiriting experience, especially when your solicitor sends you his bill for all that he has done.

400 Why should I pay the solicitor if he doesn't get the money?

A. Why not? It is not his fault that the man turns out to be worthless or a rogue. You initiated the legal claim and the

179

court case; you employed the solicitor – you are liable to pay for the work that he did for you at your request.

401 You have always stressed the importance of evidence in bringing a case. Can you explain why?

A. It is one of those things that people so often overlook. Anyone who wants to make a claim against someone else – for breach of contract or for negligence or nuisance – or anything else, must be able to prove his case. Sometimes this isn't necessary because liability is admitted, and the argument turns on how much is to be paid. Sometimes again there may be such an obvious case that very little is necessary to support your contention that something was wrong; the television may have exploded; the pullover unravelled into a ball of wool; the stud dog turns out to be a pregnant bitch; the other driver crossed through a red light. But the person against whom you are making your claim is perfectly entitled to say that he denies liability and to require you to prove it. I must emphasize that this is a proper and respectable attitude to adopt; there is nothing illegal or immoral about it. So, if the case is one about defective or shoddy goods, you will almost certainly need to have an expert who can explain what went wrong and why. Should you be arguing about a garage or a car, you will have to find a vehicle examiner who can say that he has been inspecting cars, man and boy, for thirty years, and he knows all about these things. Fabrics may have to be tested, shoes likewise; and if the holiday of a lifetime was a nightmare, statements from other guests and photos are very useful – often vital if the complaint is about construction work which is denied by the tour company. Finding an expert can be difficult – and is expensive; if you win, you will usually get his fees and expenses added to the bill, which the loser will pay (you hope).

402 Recently I had an argument in a shop about what had been said by the assistant when I was buying. The upshot was

that I was told that it was 'just your word against ours'. Does this mean that I have no case?

A. Not at all; your word is extremely good evidence of what happened. Sometimes defendants don't realize this basic situation; if you claim that something is defective; that the salesman made statements about it prior to your purchase; that your claim is denied; that you sue and finally end up in the witness box telling the judge about it, then – unless you are a liar, thief, cheat or crook – the chances are that you will be believed. The judge will say to himself that you would not have gone through this tedious rigmarole just for fun or to annoy the trader. So, in the absence of anything in writing, your word is very acceptable as evidence in support of your case.

403 A man who drove into my car immediately admitted liability, said how sorry he was, and told me to send him the bill. I did, and he was abusive and hostile saying that I was making it up. What can I do?

A. Again the same principle applies. Go to court and tell your side of the story – including the other driver's admission. I expect he denied it later because his insurers jumped down his throat – a cardinal rule of hoping to shelter behind an insurance policy is never to admit anything at all.

404 Is there any alternative to suing, going to court, that is?

A. Yes, in some cases. Traders who belong to a number of trade associations which have agreed Codes of Practice with the Office of Fair Trading will usually agree to the dispute being sorted out by *arbitration*. Normally arbitration is almost the same as a court case, except that it is quicker. Both parties choose a person to act as arbitrator and then use lawyers and put their cases in writing, finally attending a hearing with witnesses. But for these Codes of Practice a low cost form of arbitration has been approved. The administration will be by the Institute of Arbitrators; which appoints an arbitrator. Both sides put their case in writing and each can comment, in writing, on what the other says. The arbitrator then reads all the written submissions and any other documents involved, and makes up his mind without seeing either side. This method does save costs and time, but sometimes the people involved may feel that the result is not quite what they hoped, and there may be an impression that one has been cheated of one's day in court! Arbitrators, in dealing with these low-cost documents-only arbitrations, will try to be fair to both sides, as well as applying principles of law, of course. Fairness may result in a compromise solution rather than the judgment a court might have awarded. This may be perfectly satisfactory as a small claim settling scheme – so long as those who are expected to take part realize it.

405 Are there cases where arbitration is the only answer?

A. Insurance policies commonly provide for disputes to be dealt with by arbitration, as do quite a number of trade contracts. This is growing, too, because an *arbitration clause* is not capable of being challenged as an unfair contract term, and some traders are realizing that arbitration may put off a potential claimant.

406 I am a trader dealing in mail order. As such, I rely heavily on my suppliers, and if one lets me down, I may be unable to supply my customers. This can result in cash-flow problems, and I have a fear of being caught in-between – unable to supply the goods or refund the money. Is there any suggestion you can make to help protect my customers, who often have to wait a long time for the goods?

A. What a very sensible trader you must be. One of the most ordered common complaints is about paying in advance for goods through mail order or magazines, and receiving

182

neither the goods nor a refund. So, anything that can end this practice is to be warmly welcomed. The simplest thing is for the trader to open a special bank account into which all pre-payments are put. They sit there until the goods are ready and despatched. Then the trader pays himself by transferring the price from the special account to his own. Should he go bust in between, the money in the special account will be treated as still belonging to the customers who paid it, and they will get their money back in full.

407 Say the worst does happen and the trader becomes insolvent, what should a consumer who is owed money or hasn't received goods do to help himself?

A. You will be a *creditor* in the bankruptcy or the liquidation. The first thing is to inform the person appointed to look after the affairs of the trader – the trustee-in-bankruptcy or the liquidator. Write (keeping a copy) informing him of the extent of the debt owed to you. If you receive no reply – and some of these people are far too slow in dealing with correspondence, or if you cannot find out who the person is, you could get in touch with the Official Receiver – a government officer whose job it is to tackle the immediate results of an insolvency. You can find him under 'Trade, Department of' in the phone book, and his office should be able to tell you the name and address of the trustee or liquidator; and he will try and persuade someone to deal with your complaint. BUT – blood and stones again – if there are no assets or heavy debts, the chances of getting any money are slim and there is likely to be a very long wait. So don't expect miracles.

408 I keep being told that I owe some money to a trader. He sends me letters saying that if I don't pay, he will sue me and tell my boss and family. I do not believe that I am in debt because the money which was outstanding has all been paid. What can I do?

A. First, it is an offence (Section 40, Administration of Justice Act 1970) to harass a person demanding money, or to make threats of publicity about the debt, which is calculated to alarm, distress, or humiliate him or his family. So, you could go to the police and ask them to take action against the trader – pointing out that this *is* a criminal matter. Or you could ask the trading standards department or the solicitor's department of your local council to consider taking action under its powers (Section 222, Local Government Act 1972). Secondly, you could inform the Office of Fair Trading (see page 206), because the trader's action could put at risk any licence he has been granted under the Consumer Credit Act 1974. Thirdly, there is provision under Section 103 of that Act which enables you to ask for a statement either confirming that you have paid up in full or setting out what is still due. Finally, you could write to the trader (keeping a copy) saying you do not owe a penny, and if he sues you, the action will be defended. Remind him also of the crime of harassment.

409 I have been paying back a loan and interest to a money-lender. Although I borrowed £500, I have had to pay far more than that and I still owe money. It seems to go on for ever. Is there any way that I can call a halt to this continuous drain?

A. The Consumer Credit Act 1974 has a very valuable provision dealing with what it calls *extortionate credit bargains* in Section 137. The Act enables you to go to the court and ask for the credit bargain to be reopened 'so as to do justice between the parties'. A credit bargain is extortionate if you have to pay sums which are *grossly exorbitant*, or which contravene *ordinary principles of fair dealing*. You can take any agreement to the court – not simply hire-purchase ones, but those made with a money-lender, a mortgage company, fringe bank, and even family arrangements. And it doesn't matter when the agreement was made – as long as it is not more than six years since you made the last payment. This is a very good measure of protection and is well worth

184

invoking, either on your own, or if you are taken to court by someone claiming money, or, say, served with a possession order on any house which was taken as security.

410 I think my solicitor is incompetent; he is slow in dealing with letters and does not explain what is going on. Can I change to someone else?

A. Yes, of course you can, but you will have to pay the first solicitor before he will release the papers to the next one. Why don't you make an appointment and go and see him? Tell him what you think about his competence, and see what his explanation is. There are very often good reasons for doing nothing which any solicitor will recognize, but which the client will think is just time wasting unless it is explained to him. Each time a solicitor writes to you, more costs are incurred, and he may actually be trying to do you a favour by not writing.

411 Is there anyone who can help me? My solicitor has been negligent.

A. I wonder if he has? I am not for a moment trying to defend him, but just pointing out that the public's idea of negligence is often far from the way a lawyer sees it. If he *has* been negligent, you can only turn to another solicitor to take on the case which the first chap has mishandled and to see if you have any redress against him. Don't think you can write to The Law Society – the solicitors' professional body – because they can only act if the solicitor has broken the rules – by making off with your money, or being unduly slow in dealing with your case, or has acted unprofessionally. They have no power to interfere with allegations of negligence. I know they may seem unhelpful, but that is the way it is, and will remain until the recommendations of the Royal Commission on Legal Services are implemented.

412 Can you explain about legal aid?

A. I will try. It is difficult enough for a solicitor to understand; that much harder for you. There are two types – civil and criminal. Criminal legal aid is dealt with by magistrates court and the Crown Courts and is discussed in question 435. Civil legal aid is in two parts – *Green Form* and *Legal Aid.*

413 What is *Green Form*?

A. This is a scheme which provides for £25 worth of legal help for virtually anything you can think of in the legal field – housing, divorce, welfare rights, accidents, wills, crime, your job; its only limitation is that your solicitor cannot go into court and speak for you on Green Form. But he can do everything else, interview you and other witnesses, write letters, prepare documents, until he has used up £25 worth of time. He can ask The Law Society to increase that limit – and this can be done up to, say, £50, depending on the type of case.

414 How does one get Green Form help?

A. There is a simple form which the solicitor will fill in which contains details of your savings and income. A means test is used, and your chances of qualifying depend as well on the number of dependants you have. The financial contributions are changed each November, so the figures quoted may be a guide only. If you are single with no dependants, the savings limit is £600. More savings – no Green Form help. If you have dependants, £200 savings is allowed for the first, £120 for the second, and £60 for the third and subsequent ones. Again, if the limit is exceeded – no Green Form. This can mean that even a person on Supplementary Benefit or Family Income Supplement who has larger savings than the limit will not get Green Form help.

415 What about income?

A. Again, this depends on the dependants you have as well as on what your income is. If you get Supplementary Benefit or Family Income Supplement, you automatically qualify for Green Form unless your savings are too high (see above). Apart from that, the solicitor takes your gross income, deducts your income tax and National Insurance contributions (but not other payments you make) – and so much for each dependant – £9.70 for spouse, and a sliding scale for children depending on their age. BUT unless your spouse is the cause of your getting legal help, her income is also taken into account, with the result that most working couples are outside Green Form unless it's for divorce or maintenance. So far, so good. The figure that is left after these deductions have been made is called the *disposable income*. If that is more than £35 a week you will be asked to pay a contribution to the solicitor. This is on a sliding scale – £11 if your disposable income is £44; £50 if it is £70. The upper limit for disposable income is £75 – over that you are outside Green Form. The odd thing about it is that many people will fail to get Green Form, but still qualify for Legal Aid. But always ask the solicitor to do the sums, it may well be worth it.

416 Is *Legal Aid* worked out on the same basis? You hear about rich people getting it while hard up ones don't.

A. Legal Aid proper is to enable you to take or defend proceedings in the county court or the High Court (and in magistrates courts for family matters, the Crown Court on appeal in these cases, and The Lands Tribunal). It is NOT available for libel cases or for you to be represented by a solicitor in any other tribunal case. Again, it is a means-tested benefit, but the assessment enables a lot more to be taken off to determine the *disposable income* – mortgage repayments, rent, h.p. debts, rates, insurance, maintenance payments, as well as tax and N.I. contributions – and allowances for dependants. Capital calculations are also made, and you may have to pay a contribution out of your savings as well as from your income. All types of legal aid work against the thrifty.

417 What are the limits for Legal Aid?

A. At present, if your *disposable income* is less than £1500, Legal Aid is free; over £3,600, you don't get it. In between you may have to pay a contribution of £1 for every £4 above £1500 – so, if your disposable income comes out at £2500, you find out the contribution by deducting the £1500 – leaving £1000; one-quarter of that = £250, which is your contribution payable by twelve equal instalments. Deductions for yourself and dependants are made from your savings leaving a figure of *disposable capital*. If it is less than £1200, you don't have to pay any of it; but if it is between £1200 and £2500, you have to pay the whole amount above £1200 as a contribution. Over £2500 you are outside Legal Aid.

418 I still do not see how some people earning large sums can get Legal Aid.

A. Because they probably have lots of outgoings, and large families. Two wives, a handful of children, mortgages, rates, insurance and other debts, plus maintenance, can mean that one can earn £10,000 or more and still get free legal aid. The unfairness returns when one's spouse also works. This makes it difficult for some people to get Legal Aid for accident claims, for example.

419 Assuming I pay a contribution of one kind or another to The Law Society, what happens if I win my case?

A. If you are awarded money by the court and are awarded costs as well, and the loser pays both *those*, then eventually you will get most of your contributions back. Not all,
188

because of the way solicitors' costs work – part of those costs are not payable by the loser; this part will come out of your contribution.

420 Is this bound to result in a repayment to me?

A. Only if you win AND get paid – blood and stones again! If the loser doesn't pay the money or costs, you won't get your contribution back. This may seem hard, but if you did you would be in a better position than the person who paid for his solicitor himself. Another point to remember is that the compensation or damages that the court awards you has to be paid to The Law Society, and can be used in part payment of your costs. So, don't celebrate until the cheque comes through the door.

421 Surely, if I lose, I will have to pay the winner's legal costs? I don't have the money – that is why I am on legal aid. Can I be forced to?

A. The usual order is that the loser who is legally aided should not have to pay the winner more than the amount of the contributions which he paid as a condition of legal aid. If you didn't have a contribution – what is sometimes called a *nil certificate* – you won't have to pay the winner anything.

422 How does The Law Society deal with legal aid applications?

A. The person applying completes an application form. This may be a bit complicated, so you can ask your solicitor to help you on Green Form. It is sent to The Law Society's local legal aid office. The financial assessment is dealt with by the Supplementary Benefits Commission, who inform the Law Society whether you come within the scope of the money limits. If you do, The Law Society considers the legal merits of your

189

case and decides whether or not to offer you a *legal aid certificate*. If they do, you will receive a form asking you if you want legal aid, and setting out the terms and conditions – contributions, limitations, and so on. You decide, and if you accept, you sign the form and send it back. A legal aid certificate is sent out a few days later. Should The Law Society think that you haven't got a good case, or that the benefit you will achieve is not worth the cost of pursuing it, or if you are outside the financial scope, you will be sent a notice of refusal of legal aid. There is a form of appeal against this, and your solicitor can help you with it under Green Form.

423 Who pays for the work which the solicitor does before the legal aid certificate is granted?

A. Unless you are getting Green Form help – YOU PAY. So, do be careful about getting your solicitor to do anything until you know your legal aid position.

424 Does the £25 limit on Green Form apply to divorce, and can I get Legal Aid for that?

A. There are special rules about Legal Aid and divorce. First, the Green Form upper limit of solicitors' work is £45 – so that you can get a considerable amount of work done on the same financial test. Secondly, Legal Aid is NOT available to take divorce proceedings. So, the procedure of actually ending the marriage is not covered by Legal Aid, although Green Form help and advice – for completing the forms and understanding what has to be done – is available up to £45 worth of work. Legal Aid IS offered for all matters relating to children, maintenance, property and the sorting out of all other aspects of the broken marriage. Legal Aid IS available, too, if the divorce becomes contested, or if (exceptionally) the court directs a hearing in open court, if the applicant can't deal with the matter on his own because of physical or mental handicap – as well as for applying for an *injunction* or to bring the divorce within three years from the marriage.

425 Can legal aid be applied for by a child?

A. As a child – with help from a parent or guardian – can be a party to court proceedings, so he can apply for legal aid. Where he is under sixteen and is being fully maintained by an adult, the adult's means will be used to determine financial eligibility.

426 How long does it take to get a legal aid certificate?

A. Usually the process takes about eight weeks. A lot depends on your co-operation with the Legal Aid Assessment office and on how complicated your legal case is.

427 Is it possible to speed up the process?

A. If a sudden problem arises – you are a battered woman, or a bulldozer is about to knock your house down – an urgent application to a court may be needed. If you are within legal aid limits, your solicitor can ask The Law Society – by phone if necessary – for an *emergency certificate*. While this will cover the work that has to be done in a hurry, you have to promise to pay whatever contributions may be assessed – and if you have savings, these may be much higher than you (or your solicitor) might imagine.

428 If I am involved in a court case and my opponent is legally aided, can I get an order for costs against the Legal Aid Fund if I win?

A. There are severe limitations. The legally aided person *must* have started the proceedings, and you will have to show that you would suffer severe financial hardship unless the order was made. It is, therefore, rarely done, but is worth bearing in mind to tell your solicitor about – just in case you qualify.

429 You have mentioned that sometimes money awarded to a person can be retained by The Law Society. How can this be? I thought the idea was to help you win, not keep your winnings.

A. It is what is called the *statutory charge*. The Law Society which administers civil legal aid for the Government is really lending you money to pay for your solicitor. It is thought fair, therefore, that if you win, at least some of your winnings should repay this loan. The worst effect of the use of the *statutory charge* is where the legally aided person wins but doesn't get awarded costs, or can't recover the costs. Where a losing party is ordered to pay by small instalments, these are just sent to The Law Society until the costs have been paid; then they start coming to you – often years later. There are some exemptions: for small payments in magistrates courts; for the first £2500 of the value of property recovered (which means either a lump sum in cash, or, say, a share of a house) in matrimonial proceedings; or under an award made after a person's death for a share of his estate. But don't think that this charge doesn't mean anything. It does; it is like a mortgage. It is payable to The Law Society as a first charge, although it may be deferred until a house is sold. So, you should ensure that your solicitor explains to you what the effect of this will be – and you should also take into account the need to apply for an order for costs to try and stop the money being eroded further. The longer and more bitter the battle after a divorce for example, the higher the costs, and the more expensive it may be in the end – even though you 'win'.

430 I have a query on the bill which my solicitor has sent me. It seems far too high to me, and I don't understand what his explanation means. How can I resolve this and get it reduced?

A. First of all, go and see him. Tell him your worries and ask for an explanation. Secondly, many people don't realize that, as long as you are with a solicitor, or talking to him over the phone, the 'meter is running'. You will find these items reflected in his bill. Many people, too, simply do not know the high cost of the actual phone calls which the solicitor may make. The cost of a long distance STD phone call lasting fifteen minutes in the morning is 97.2p; this will be added to the solicitor's fee. If you have a full explanation of the time spent and letters written, as well as phone calls, etc., you may be satisfied.

431 How do solicitors work out their costs and charges?

A. I wish I could be more helpful on this. Solicitors ought to stick up a list of their charges in their waiting rooms, so that every client can know in advance roughly what they will be charged. Most firms use an hourly rate which varies from £10–£12 in small offices (with low overheads) to £25–£35 or more for the large City firms. Some add on the cost of letters and phone calls at £2 or £3 a go.The best advice is ASK beforehand. V.A.T. is charged on top of the bill.

432 Does this have any bearing on Green Form advice?

A. Yes, it does; the scheme provides for £25 worth (or £45 worth in divorce cases) of the solicitor's time. So, if he is charging £33 an hour, you won't get more than a few minutes! For legal aid work the average rate is about £13 per hour, so that the Green Form ought to get you a couple of hours. In some parts of the country solicitors may charge less than this – again ASK.

433 And if I cannot agree a figure for costs, what then?

A. You can do one of two things. If the case has nothing to do with a court, you can ask the solicitor to obtain a *remu-*

neration certificate from The Law Society. This involves each of you making comments on the size of the bill, and an official at The Law Society will determine what is a fair charge. The solicitor almost always abides by this assessment. It has the great advantage of being free. In any other case, you can ask for the bill to be assessed (*taxed*) by a court. This costs money, and if you don't get the bill reduced by much, you will have to pay the costs of the solicitor for dealing with this assessment – so you may end up worse off. If you are legally aided, the solicitor's bill will almost always be *taxed* by the court.

434 Who is the Lay Observer?

A. He is a person appointed by the Lord Chancellor to look into complaints that The Law Society has not dealt properly with complaints made to it about solicitors. So you can see that he has a very limited function indeed. His office is in the Law Courts, and you can approach him only after you have been through the hands of the Law Society.

435 What is 'criminal legal aid'?

A. This is quite separate from civil legal aid, and is administered by the Home Office. The Law Society is not directly involved, except that the legal aid fund pays the costs of criminal legal aid in magistrates courts. *Criminal legal aid* covers the solicitor's work in representing a person accused of a crime; also, it may meet a barrister's fees. It is only available AFTER you have been accused of a crime; before that you must rely on *Green Form*. You apply for criminal legal aid at the court by completing a form. A means test is applied, and the clerk to the court or the court itself may grant legal aid if it is satisfied that the interests of justice show that it ought to be granted and that your means are such that you need help to pay the cost of defending yourself. There are no financial limits as such, but a contribution may often be required. The more serious the offence, the more likely it is that criminal legal aid will be granted.

436 Is there anything that can be done when mortgage arrears occur? I have been in financial difficulties following lay-offs in my employment, and, although I have struggled, I can't keep up the full payments.

A. Immediately you have read this answer, go to the building society branch office, see the manager, and explain to him what your problems are. Don't wait for a premium bond to come up – go now. The building society, like any other creditor, will assume that shortfalls are due to lack of inclination UNLESS you tell them. So, if your money falls, you are on short-time, unemployed, or if your marriage has broken down – tell the society. The manager is human, he knows that things can go wrong and will do what he can to help you, by reducing the payments, extending the mortgage term, or suggesting that you sell the house to buy a cheaper one, or change your mortgage to an *option mortgage*. He may also suggest that there are benefits for which you may qualify from the Social Security. This is the best advice I can give. If you do nothing, there will very likely be court proceedings for possession, which will add to the expenses you already face.

437 What sort of financial help may I get?

A. Are you claiming all the tax allowances you are entitled to? If you earn a low wage, you may qualify for *Family Income Supplement*. *Rate Rebates* are also available if you are having money troubles. If you don't work, you may well be able to claim *Supplementary Benefit*, and this will mean a payment in addition for the interest part of the mortgage instalments, and an annual allowance for repairs and insurance. If you have a second mortgage, the interest on this will probably be paid, too.

438 I am a tenant, so can I get any of these benefits paid to me?

A. You won't get mortgage help, of course; but the other benefits mentioned, including Rent Rebates, may well apply to you.

439 How can I find out about benefits generally?

A. There are a considerable number of family benefits, sickness payments and so on, and often qualifying for one – like Family Income Supplement or Supplementary Benefit, for example – may act as a passport to other help, like free school meals, milk, dentists' bills and glasses. The golden rule for all Social Security benefits is; ASK. You will get it if you qualify, but no one will come round and offer you money. And don't think that you are accepting charity; it is a right for which you have contributed, often for many years. Leaflets and booklets are available free from Social Security offices.

440 I don't understand the way in which my benefit has been calculated, and no one seems to be able to explain it to me.

A. You should ask in writing for a *Notice of Assessment* (Form A 124), which will explain how your benefit has been worked out. If you think the figure is wrong, you can appeal. You may need legal help on the Green Form or from a Rights Centre, Law Centre, Citizens Advice Centre, or the Child Poverty Action Group (see page 205).

441 Is there any way of seeing a solicitor cheaply or without paying at all?

A. If you qualify for Green Form (see question 413) without any contribution, your legal advice *is* free. Apart from that, there is a scheme called the *Fixed Fee Interview* in which a very large number of solicitors participate. Under this scheme you can have half-an-hour's advice from a solicitor – whose name you can obtain from the Legal Aid Referral List – and it will not cost you more than £5 including V.A.T. The Fixed Fee Interview will cover any legal topic you want to discuss – so do make use of it.

442 Can I get hold of a solicitor in an emergency?

A. In the Legal Aid Referral List there is a list of solicitors who can be contacted out of office hours in urgent cases.

GLOSSARY

Access the right of the parent with whom children do not live to see them and to have them to stay from time to time.

Adoption order a legal transference of the rights and duties of the natural parent to another person.

Affidavit a sworn statement in writing containing facts or evidence; it is witnessed by a solicitor or (in divorce or county court cases) a court officer.

Arbitration a method of resolving disputes without going through a court, each party agreeing to an independent person to adjudicate on the problem; also – an informal low-cost way of dealing with small claims in the county court.

Bailment the transfer of possession of goods without change of ownership.

Bankruptcy what happens when an individual becomes insolvent or unable to pay his debts.

Bridging loan a temporary loan, usually from a bank, to help with raising the money to buy a house until a mortgage comes through.

Bye-law a regulation made by the local council having the rule of law in the district.

Codicil an additional supplement to a will.

Commitment fee a charge made by a bank for a loan, especially for a bridging loan.

Common-law wife a lady with whom a man lives but to whom he is not married.

Completion the moment when the deeds of a house are handed over in exchange for the money.

Contributory negligence an off-set to compensation because of the victim's own action in causing or making worse the injury sustained.

Conveyancing the process of the legal transfer of the title to land.

County court a local court dealing with divorce and most other matters relating to disputes up to a financial limit (generally £2000 at present).

Covenants clauses in deeds relating to land in which someone promises to do (or not to do) something.

Credit-sale a form of selling on credit terms where the ownership of the goods changes hands immediately and they become the property of the buyer.

Creditor someone who is owed money.

Custody the right of a parent after a court order to make major decisions about a child's future.

Damages an award of compensation for death or injury, or for a breach of contract.

Debtor a person who owes money.

Decree absolute the final order of a court ending a marriage, after which one can remarry.

Decree nisi the first order ending a marriage, but which does not enable one to remarry.

Disbursements the expenses and out-of-pocket payments made by a solicitor on his client's behalf.

Domicile the country in which a person resides permanently.

Evidence information which supports facts in dispute.

199

Exclusion clause a term in a contract or in a notice by which a person tries to limit or avoid his liability to others for negligence or breach of contract.

Executor the person named in a will whose job it is to collect the assets and pay the debts.

Green Form a type of free or low cost legal advice available from solicitors.

Guarantee a document issued with many goods in which the manufacturer undertakes to repair goods (subject to conditions) within a limited time.

Hire-purchase a form of selling on credit where the ownership of the goods remains with someone other than the buyer until the last payment.

Implied terms undertakings as to description, quality and fitness for purpose automatically included in every contract for the sale of goods because of the Sale of Goods Act (they are also found in many other contracts).

Injunction a court order forbidding someone from interfering with one's legal rights; also an order making one do something.

Intestate a person who dies without leaving a will.

Joint tenancy a form of joint ownership where the survivor takes everything.

Land charge some charge or mortgage affecting land; also certain court orders and bankruptcy.

Land Registry the government office which contains details of titles to land which is registered.

Lease a document transferring temporary ownership of land usually for a long period of years, for which the occupier pays rent to a landlord.

Legal Aid a scheme providing free or low cost help for people bringing or defending court cases.

Letters of administration the document issued to the person administering the estate of a person who dies without a will appointing executors.

Liquidation what happens when a limited company becomes insolvent or is unable to pay its debts.

Material fact information which must be disclosed to an insurance company before it takes on a risk.

Mortgage a document pledging land as security for a loan.

Mortgagee the person who lends money on mortgage.

Mortgagor the person who borrows money on mortgage.

Negligence the breach of a duty of care owed to another person; doing some act which a reasonable person would not do – or not doing what a reasonable person would have done.

Nuisance interfering with a person's use and enjoyment of his land or property.

Nullity a situation arising when a marriage is void, or voidable.

Option mortgage a method of borrowing money on a mortgage where the rate of interest payable is kept low in exchange for going without tax allowances.

Overriding interests matters affecting land which are not shown on the land register.

Personal representative a person to whom a grant of letters of administration is made when a person dies without leaving a will or an executor.

Petition the formal document in which the facts about a marriage are contained to lead to a divorce.

Petitioner the person who starts divorce proceedings.

Probate the formal document issued by the court to an executor after a will has been proved.

Receiver a person appointed to look after the affairs of a mentally ill patient; or someone who takes over a limited company when it is in financial trouble.

Respondent the person against whom divorce proceedings are taken.

Retention money kept back from a mortgage until work is done to a house.

Spent convictions criminal offences which are treated as forgotten after a certain period of time.

Stamp duty a tax payable by a person who buys land or a house or who takes on a lease.

Statutory declaration a written statement of facts which is witnessed before a solicitor.

Subject to contract a form of words used to ensure that there is no binding legal contract between the seller and buyer of land.

Tenancy-in-common a form of joint ownership where each person has an undivided share which does not pass to the survivor (see joint tenancy).

Testator a person who makes a will.

Trespass infringement of legal rights over land and property by a person without permission.

Trustee-in-bankruptcy a person appointed to administer the affairs of a bankrupt individual.

Unfair dismissal having one's job ended in a way which gives rise to a right to go to an industrial tribunal.

Vendor a person who is selling something (usually land or a house).

Ward of court a child whose custody is vested in the court; usually made when it is feared that a child will be 'snatched' or taken abroad. It continues until the child attains eighteen.

Wrongful dismissal having one's job ended in a way which entitles one to sue for damages in the courts for breach of contract.

WHERE TO GO FOR HELP AND FURTHER INFORMATION

GENERAL

Citizens' Advice Bureau – over 700 in Britain – see phone book under 'C'.

Consumer Advice Centre – over 120 – ask at a public library, town hall or Trading Standards Department – also try the phone book under the name of your local Council or County Council.

County court – see phone book under 'C' for Court.

Law Centre – only eighteen in London and nine others, in Birmingham, Cardiff, Coventry, Liverpool, Manchester, Merthyr, Newcastle; addresses from Legal Action Group (see p. 205) or a library, town hall or the police.

Magistrates court – see phone book under 'C' for Court or ask the police.

Public library – see phone book under your local council.

Solicitors – look in classified section of phone book or Yellow Pages for a general list – under 'S' for solicitor. For details of solicitors who do legal aid work, and give a 'Fixed fee interview' – see the LEGAL AID REFERRAL LIST at libraries, advice centres, town halls and police stations. For information about LEGAL AID see phone book under 'L' for Law Society.

Town Hall Information Office

OTHER ADDRESSES

Advertising Standards Authority, 15 Ridgmount Street, London WC1.

British Insurance Association, Aldermary House, Queen Street, London EC4.

Capital Taxes Offices (for Capital Transfer Tax), Lynwood Road, Thames Ditton, Surrey, (01-398-4242) for transfers in lifetime;

Rockley Road, London W14 (01-603-4622) for transfers on death. Forms and booklets available.

Child Poverty Action Group (C.P.A.G.), 1 Macklin Street, London WC2. C.P.A.G. campaigns for the badly-off and produces extremely low-priced handbooks and information sheets on the whole range of benefits and allowances – and welcomes subscribers.

Companies Registry and **Registry of Business Names**, City Road, London EC1 (01-253-9393); also Crown Way, Maindy, Cardiff.

Consumers' Association, 14 Buckingham Street, London WC2, publishers of '*Which?*' magazines.

Court of Protection, 25 Store Street, London WC1.

Divorce Registry, Somerset House, Strand, London, WC2 – also divorce county courts under 'C' for court in the phone book.

Equal Opportunities Commission, Quay Street, Manchester (01-833-9244).

Income Tax problems – P.A.Y.E. enquiry offices are in London and seven other places in England. Your own tax inspector will be able to help; any other tax office will either help or put you on to the right tax office. See under 'Inland Revenue' in the phone book.

Land Charges Registry, Burrington Way, Plymouth.

Land Registry – main office is in Lincolns' Inn Fields, London WC2; there are also District Offices throughout the country.

Law Society, 113 Chancery Lane, London WC2 (01-242-1222).

Legal Action Group, 28a Highgate Road, London NW5.

London Small Claims Court, 235–328 High Holborn, London WC1 (01-242-8531) provides a cheap, quick and informal method of resolving small claims (£10–£350).

205

Low Pay Unit, 1 Macklin Street, London WC2.

Mechanical Copyright Protection Society Ltd, 380 Streatham High Road, London SW16 (01-769-3181).

Motor Insurers Bureau (M.I.B.), Aldermary House, Queen Street, London EC4 (01-248-4477).

National Council for Civil Liberties (N.C.C.L.), 186 Kings Cross Road, London WC1.

National Council for One-Parent Familes, 255 Kentish Town Road, London NW5.

Office of Fair Trading, Breams Buildings, London EC4.

Official Receivers in Companies Liquidation, Atlantic House, Holborn Viaduct, London EC1.

Official Receivers in Bankruptcy (High Court), Thomas More Building, Royal Courts of Justice, London WC2. For local offices see the phone book under 'Trade, Dept of'.

Ombudsman (Parliamentary Commissioner and Health Service Commissioner's office), Church House, Great Smith Street, London SW1.

Performing Rights Society Ltd, 29 Berners Street, London W1 (01-580-5544).

Probate and Wills:
a **Register of Wills** deposited for safe custody; write to Senior Registrar, Family Division, Somerset House, Strand, London WC2.
b **Inspection of wills,** probate and letters of administration; Probate Registry Search Section, Somerset House, Strand, London WC2.
c **Personal Application Department,** 4th floor, Adelphi Building, John Adam Street, Strand, London WC2 (01-217-5046).
d For **local Probate Registries:** Birmingham, Bodmin, Brighton, Bristol, Carlisle, Chester, Exeter, Gloucester, Hull, Ipswich, Lancaster, Leeds, Leicester, Lincoln, Liverpool, Maidstone, Manchester, Middlesbrough, Newcastle, Norwich, Notting-

ham, Oxford, Peterborough, Sheffield, Stoke-on-Trent, Winchester, York.

e Welsh District Probate Registries: Bangor, Carmarthen, Llandaff.

Registrar-General of Births, Marriages and Deaths, St Catherine's House, Aldwych, London WC2.

Trading Standards Departments (also called Consumer Protection or Weights and Measures Inspectors) ask at the town hall or local library.

V.A.T. problems and registration: see the phone book under 'C' for Customs and Excise; or Kings Beam House, London EC4.

Wages Council Inspectorate – on a regional basis. See the phone book under 'W' for Wages Inspectorate or ask at a Jobcentre, Employment Office or the Department of Employment, 8 St James's Square, London SW1.

USEFUL PUBLICATIONS

Accidents
Accidents and the Law by Neville D. Vandyk; Oyez Publishing Ltd, £1.50.

Benefits
D.H.S.S. leaflets and booklets; free from most Social Security offices or obtain the complete *Catalogue* from Leaflets Section, D.H.S.S., Honeypot Lane, Edgware, Middlesex.

National Welfare Benefits Handbook; published each year by the Child Poverty Action Group, 1 Macklin Street, London WC2, about 75p plus postage.

Conveyancing
Introduction to Conveyancing by Edward Moeran; Oyez Publishing Ltd, £4.95.

The Legal Side of Buying a House; Consumers' Association, Caxton Hill, Hertford, £2.25.

Courts
How to Sue in the County Court; Consumers' Association, Caxton Hill, Hertford, £2.

Small Claims in the County Court; *free* from any county court.

Divorce
Acting in Person; Oyez Publishing Ltd, £6.75 (also available by post from Oyez, Freepost, SE1).

On Getting Divorced; Consumers' Association, Caxton Hill, Hertford, £2.25.

Undefended Divorce; *free* booklet from any divorce County Court or Somerset House.

Employment
Dismissal, Redundancy and Job-hunting; Consumers' Association, Caxton Hill, Hertford, £1.75.

Employment Protection; a series of *free* leaflets on job rights from any Jobcentre or Employment Office.

Employment Protection (Consolidation) Act 1978 by Brian Bercusson; Sweet & Maxwell, about £3.50.

Mind Your Own Staff; D.I.T.B., Maclaren House, Talbot Road, Stretford, Manchester, about £1.

General

The Buyer's Right; Consumers' Association, Caxton Hill, Hertford, £3.45.

Civil Liberty: The N.C.C.L. Guide; Penguin, £1.75.

Claiming on Home, Car and Holiday Insurance; Consumers' Association, Caxton Hill, Hertford, £1.75.

Consumers – Know your Rights by John Harries; Oyez Publishing Ltd, £3.95.

Consumer Law; Sweet & Maxwell, about £8.50.

Consumers and the Law by Ross Cranston; Weidenfeld & Nicolson, £7.95 (paperback).

The Consumer, Society and the Law by Borrie and Diamond; Penguin Books, £1.

Treatment and Care in Mental Illness; Consumers' Association, Caxton Hill, Hertford, £1.50.

Legal Aid

Legal Aid Guide; *free* from the The Law Society's legal aid offices.

Legal Aid Leaflet; *free* from libraries and advice centres.

Legal Aid Summary by Edward Moeran; Oyez Publishing Ltd, £1.95.

Tax

Free leaflets and booklets from any tax office or from Inland Revenue, Somerset House, Strand, London WC2, on: *Income Tax and One Parent Families; Income Tax – Separation and Divorce; Starting in Business; Capital Gains Tax; Capital Transfer Tax.*

Wills

A Probate Handbook by D. R. Holloway; Oyez Publishing Ltd, £7.50.

What To Do When Someone Dies; Consumers' Association, Caxton Hill, Hertford, £1.75.

Wills and Probate; Consumers' Association, Caxton Hill, Hertford, £2.

INDEX

(all references are to question numbers)

210

211

213

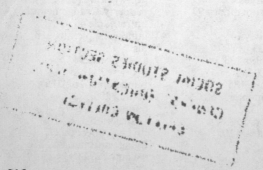